PORTRAIT OF A
DANISH CONMAN

To Anette

PORTRAIT OF A DANISH CONMAN

Otto Stein – *Framed within the Life and Novels of his Creator, Jacob Paludan*

FRANTZ LEANDER HANSEN

Translated from Danish by Gaye Kynoch

sussex
ACADEMIC
PRESS
Brighton • Chicago • Toronto

Copyright © Frantz Leander Hansen, 2021.

The right of Frantz Leander Hansen to be identified as Author of this work, and Gaye Kynoch as Translator, has been asserted in accordance with the Copyright, Designs and Patents Act 1988.

2 4 6 8 10 9 7 5 3 1

First published in Danish by Museum Tusculanum Press, Copenhagen, 2018.
Published in English, 2021, in Great Britain by
SUSSEX ACADEMIC PRESS
PO Box 139
Eastbourne BN24 9BP

Distributed in North America by
SUSSEX ACADEMIC PRESS
Independent Publishers Group
814 N. Franklin Street, Chicago, IL 60610

All rights reserved. Except for the quotation of short passages for the purposes of criticism and review, no part of this publication may be reproduced, stored in a retrieval system, or transmitted, in any form or by any means, electronic, mechanical, photocopying, recording or otherwise, without the prior permission of the publisher.

British Library Cataloguing in Publication Data
A CIP catalogue record for this book is available from the British Library.

Library of Congress Cataloguing-in-Publication Data
To be applied for.

Paperback ISBN 978-1-78976-089-7

Typeset & designed by Sussex Academic Press, Brighton & Eastbourne.
Printed TJ Books Limited, Padstow, Cornwall.

Contents

Preface	vii
Acknowledgements	xi
The Cover Illustration	xiii
The Danish Author, Jacob Paludan	xiv

Part I Routes to the Marsh Pool

Otto's final step	1
Dinner and death	2
Kinships	4
Familial motivation	6
The lost present day	7
Boundless ambition	8
Deceit at the core – Gatsby and Grünlich	9
Fraternal choices	11
Implicit faith	12
Otto and the narrator	13
Angel from the past	15
Princess of poverty	17
Otto's queen	18
The future as guarantor	21
The price of generosity	22
Big spender	23
The innocent conman	23
The guilty client	24
Full-blown swindle	26
The screw tightens	28
Advocate of darkness	29
Destructiveness and joie de vivre	31

Around the clock 34
Self-preservation and self-image 35
The mask drops 36
King and bull 37
The route to suicide 37
The ambivalence of escape 38
Sleuths 39
The final night 40
Death before normalisation and punishment 41
Otto and Alberti 42
Clarifications in the hinterland 43
Transit 44
Summing up 46
Otto: Rival and role model 49
Repercussions 51
From fluff to world-class 53

Part II Genesis of Otto in Jacob Paludan's Novels
The parrot and the mites 59
Suicide fish 61
The end of winter life 64
Face to face 67
Enterprising women 69
Rounding off 76

Part III Otto's Biographical Genesis
Fatherly favouritism 79
On the sidelines 82
Freedom of thought en plein air 83
A man of many talents 85
The Royal Oak 88
Rounding off 95

Epilogue 97

Notes   Bibliography   Index   103–140

Preface

For many a decade, *Jørgen Stein* (1933), a novel written by the Danish author Jacob Paludan, stared at me imperiously from its place on the bookshelf: 'Know thy classics.'

Finally taking up the challenge, I read the book. One of the storylines so enthralled me that I resolved to shed as much light on it as I possibly could: the story of Otto Stein, older brother of the eponymous protagonist Jørgen. Otto turns into a conman and ends up committing suicide. My mission was to unearth all the whys and wherefores underlying his fate: the factors that turn Otto into a cheat, the signposts on a route to suicide, the purpose of this dramatic story.

Moreover, it seemed to me that the story of the fraudster Otto Stein encompassed a fascinating characterisation of 'the conman' as such, and of circumstances facilitating deceit. In an optimistic moment, I even saw my exposition of this character type arousing interest all the way to the Fraud Squad, given that there seemed to be striking similarities with embezzlers and cases of fraud in our day.

By the same token, it occurred to me that mapping the routes leading to Otto's death would shed light on an exceptionally nuanced artistic rendering of issues surrounding suicide, which would be of interest beyond literary circles.

I saw Otto's story unfolding on a richly expansive canvas: ranging from the actual (criminal) psychological setting against the backdrop of an epoch, the 1920s, to a view of 'fraud' as a broader cultural and existential phenomenon.

At the same time, I became interested in the genesis of such a captivating fictional character. What were the component elements adding up to Otto? Had the author, Jacob Paludan, addressed anything similar in his previous novels? Did his personal experiences play a role? Had he taken inspiration from other writers? What catalytic agents of the author's day and of the past could have generated such a character? While working with these questions, I realised that the material could be of relevance for everyone interested in 'the origins of a fictional character'. A fascinating duality of straightforwardness and multifariousness rendered Otto highly illustrative, and could provide wide-ranging insight into literary genesis.

Danish literary historian and critic Hans Hertel has found a robust metaphor conjured up by Jacob Paludan in relation to the genesis of Marcel Proust's fictional characters: "No one would be in any doubt that the characters depicted are, like cars, 'assembled' out of small parts, small observations from thousands of places." An interesting metaphor indeed, adds Hans Hertel, but no successful synthesis of the parts would be achieved without "the magic of creativity".[1] In *Nøleren* (2012; The Delayer), a novel by Danish author Klaus Rifbjerg (1931–2015), artist Nikolaj Værn's magical talent is described thus:

> Nikolaj took it all in, and I'm not exaggerating if I say that when he drew an airplane, it was more of an airplane than the ones we saw in the sky. He could implant a lethal speed in the plane, a fiendish aggressiveness, reaching way beyond the norm, and at the same time he could walk out into the reed-wreathed area by the waterside and come back with a sketch of a warbler on a stem that was so lifelike you could hear the bird singing. There was always this *more*-ness about everything he did.[2]

This is an excellent picture of the essence of art, or indeed of the magic that ties the ingredients together and converts them into art. I shall endeavour to demonstrate the presence of this *more*-ness in the portrait of Otto, and show that he is thus endowed with a special status in *Jørgen Stein* – given that it is a strangely uneven novel, which I shall also illustrate in order to throw Otto into relief.

Many have observed the weighty significance of the elder brother, Otto, and it is therefore remarkable that far more has been written about his younger brother, Jørgen. I would like to redress this balance, and my first-chapter analysis of the Otto character focuses exclusively on aspects within the novel that are relevant to *his* story.

Thereafter, I shall investigate pointers in Jacob Paludan's five previous novels and in his own life story, seeds that grew into 'Otto'. The sightlines here have been extended in order to avoid a jumbled potpourri of life and work, rather to present a unified picture through full outlines of the novels. The specific aim is to depict the genesis of a character in a novel. Since, in Otto's case, this has hitherto only been addressed sporadically, tracking his origins will cast fresh retrospective light on Jacob Paludan's life and fiction writing. We can, for example, expand our understanding of Otto by looking at Herluf Nagel, a lawyer in Paludan's earlier novel *Fugle omkring Fyret* (1925; *Birds Around the Light*, 1928); and, similarly, our understanding of Nagel grows when he is seen alongside Otto. Comparison between elements in Otto's story and, for example, letters and newspaper articles written at the time *Jørgen Stein* was created, reveals previously unremarked inspiration from Jacob Paludan's life, thus placing the author and his work methods in a new light.

Otto does not actually need explanation; his story is so fundamentally riveting that it can be read for the excitement and tension alone. I will nonetheless embark upon the undertaking, in the belief that Jean-Paul Sartre has a point when he says that a novel is in fact created by the reader:

> for the literary object is a peculiar top which exists only in movement. To make it come into view a concrete act called

reading is necessary [...] When the words form under his pen, the author doubtless sees them, but he does not see them as the reader does [...] Since the creation can find its fulfilment only in reading, since the artist must entrust to another the job of carrying out what he has begun, since it is only through the consciousness of the reader that he can regard himself as essential to his work, all literary work is an appeal. To write is to make an appeal to the reader [...].[3]

As the reader of Otto's story, and as the writer of this analysis for the reader – I hereby take on Sartre's appeal.

Acknowledgements

Portrait of a Danish Conman was originally written and published in Danish. Publication of this English-language edition has been made possible by generous support from E. Lerager Larsen's Foundation, George and Emma Jorck Foundation, Raben-Levetzau Foundation, Rudersdal Municipality, Toyota-Foundation and VKR Family Foundation – my sincerest thanks for the interest shown in this project.

I would like to express my deep gratitude to Gaye Kynoch for her skilled translation and for enriching the manuscript with a wealth of ideas; it has been a most enjoyable and fascinating collaborative process. I am also very grateful to Ole Thestrup Pedersen for his expert and dedicated proofreading.

My warmest thanks to Anthony Grahame, Editorial Director, Sussex Academic Press. It has been a great pleasure and privilege to work once again with such a splendid and supportive publisher.

I owe special and heartfelt thanks to Else Mortensen for encouraging me to lecture on *Jørgen Stein*; had she not done so, this book would never have been written. My heartfelt thanks also to Gurli Møller and all the fantastic people at the literary academy in Rødovre.

I am greatly indebted to Hans Hertel for recommending the Danish edition of this book to Museum Tusculanum Press, with whom I went on to enjoy an excellent collaboration – my thanks to Marianne Alenius, Pernille Sys Hansen, Janus Bahs Jacquet and Julie Bjørchmar Kølle.

I would also like to express my profound gratitude to

Anette Halaburt, Hans Hertel and Else-Marie Buch Leander for reading the Danish manuscript and offering many highly valuable insights and suggestions.

My appreciative thanks to Kim Hansen for making important material available and to Niels Buch Leander for providing substantial technical assistance and excellent advice.

Verner Bylov Larsen, Søren Schou, Lars Tonnesen and Martin Zerlang provided inspiration, encouragement and ideas, for which I am extremely grateful.

I also wish to thank Jens Jacob Paludan for generously lending me three photographs of his father, reproduced in the book, and for his encouraging interest in the project.

For kindly providing information, help and support, I would like to thank Kristina Dyrlund, Inge Merete Kjeldgaard, Jakob Konnerup, Mette Risager, Gorm Tortzen and Birgitte Ørum.

I owe a special debt of gratitude to my parents, Else and Knud Hansen.

The Cover Illustration

På Langelinie (1923; At Langelinie) by the Danish artist Edvard Weie (1879-1943). Photograph: Torben E. Meyer / Esbjerg Kunstmuseum. Langelinie is a popular waterside promenade in Copenhagen. It is easy to imagine Otto Stein taking a stroll here; in his day, it was a fashionable place to be seen. The painting is an image of the effortless, carefree and affluent life craved by Otto and his 1920s' contemporaries. The walkers seem to be hovering; the scene has a dreamlike quality, and an ambiance of melancholy in a postwar era that has drifted from its anchorage. The figure seated on the bench acts as counterbalance; observing the passing picture, and uniting onlooker and artist.

THE DANISH AUTHOR, JACOB PALUDAN

Danish author Jacob Paludan (1896–1975) initially studied pharmacy. Having qualified in 1918, he worked as a pharmacist until 1924. In 1920 he spent six months in Ecuador, followed by six months in the United States, which he also visited in 1926. From 1929 until 1931 he ran a poultry farm not far from Copenhagen, on the main island of Zealand (Sjælland) in Denmark, after which he lived exclusively from his writing. Between 1922 and 1933 Jacob Paludan wrote six novels; he thereafter concentrated on an extensive output of essays alongside work as a reviewer and editor. *Jørgen Stein* (1933), in which 'the Danish conman' plays a central role, was the last of the six novels. Weighing in at over 650 pages and now considered a major work in the Danish literary canon, *Jørgen Stein* is a depiction of the roaring 1920s illustrated on a literary canvas of international standing.

Jacob Paludan, circa 1919. Photograph: Harald Hansen.

Part I

Routes to the Marsh Pool

Otto's final step

On a gloomy January evening in 1928, the heavily overweight 36-year-old lawyer Otto Stein is driving very slowly along a forest road north of Copenhagen, on the Danish island of Zealand. He is finding it so infinitely difficult to stop; when he does finally come to a standstill, he drags out the time in a dismal little café. He stumbles off into the forest to look for the deep marsh pool he remembers visiting in happier times. Hoping that perhaps he will *not* find it, giving him an excuse to abort his project, he nonetheless catches sight of the open water in the moonlit darkness, and sits down to write a letter in the glow of a struck match. There then follows one of the most spine-tingling passages in Danish literature:

> He walked straight out over the boggy ground. One pace before he had counted on doing so he stepped off into the deep, and it was as if his terror was exactly doubled by the miscalculation. The water was so cold it numbed him. Ripples appeared in the strip of moonlight on the surface of the water. Bubbles and a slight effervescence rose audibly to the surface.[4]

We follow him down: "Bubbles and a slight effervescence", and we too would like to have had one more step. To what use would Otto have put that step? A remnant of the life he had been counting on – because he is obviously counting his

2 Routes to the Marsh Pool

steps – or yet another chance to stop? By this stage in the novel we know that Otto's inner self has heated up to the point of explosion and, as his terror increases twofold, the numbingly cold water proves a solace.

Otto's death is also a condensed expression of the modus operandi via which he has survived. By focusing on one step at a time, he has managed to keep an extremely problematic existence up and running, but herein also lies a picture common to all humankind: we probably all think we have one more step, and it often comes as a huge surprise when this turns out not to be the case. We live in the expectation of one more Christmas or one more summer, and with a belief in yet another chance.

We will now follow Otto all the way to the marsh pool.

Dinner and death

We meet Otto in 1914 when he is a 22-year-old law student in Copenhagen. He has a two-year-older sister, Karen, and a six-year-younger brother, Jørgen.

At the start of the novel, the Stein family has gathered in the fjord town of Havnstrup. Situated on the west coast of northern Jutland (Jylland), the town is close enough to the North Sea for outings, and far enough from Aalborg, a large town on the east coast, that the young people have to move in order to attend upper secondary school there, which is what Jørgen will soon be doing.[5] Along with friends and local dignitaries, the Steins are preparing to celebrate the father of the family, Thorvald Stein, who has now been Havnstrup district governor[6] for fifteen years; the private living quarters in the governor's mansion are full of activity in preparation for the party. No criticism can be levelled at this contented, dependable and affluent home, nor at Thorvald Stein's career. He resolutely conducts himself with the dignity and composure of a royal-appointed official; his wife, Amalie Stein, puts her everything into home and children, ably seconded by daughter Karen who still lives with the family.

The Steins are at the very top of the local social ladder, and when Karen and her brothers are out and about on the streets of Havnstrup they are treated with a deference that bears out their privileged status. It would be hard to believe that this setting could produce a victim of suicide. However, the atmosphere of secure stability pervading this childhood home is also a picture of the torpid state in which Europe found itself just before a First World War, and which no one in their wildest imagination could had envisaged.

The dinner party held in the private home to celebrate the district governor's anniversary is a stylish demonstration of the carefree supremacy that has typified the Steins' milieu in Havnstrup. The dinner guests are the family's regular circle of people Otto has known for as long as he can remember. They are all there, but by the end of the novel only one is left. They are impressive and hardened party-loving men and women who like their wine, and the entire scene is awash with the natural abandon of the North Sea: "The conversation which still rose and subsided in waves, would soon resolve itself into a steady, undifferentiated hum of voices."[7] This persistent hum is the very same rumbling that will soon be thundering throughout Europe.

The young participants in the dinner party play with the idea of switching the place cards on the table, but that would be like "changing the law of gravity".[8] And then, a radical change to the natural order of things is exactly what happens during dinner when news arrives about the murders in Sarajevo: the assassination of heir to the Austro-Hungarian Empire Archduke Franz Ferdinand and his wife.

The news causes Governor Stein to ask himself how much longer this Havnstrup circle will be able to meet; the answer comes from the open window and the candles:

The curtain, caught by a sudden gust of air, billowed like a sail, and the candle flames flickered like so many squirming worms. Fru Nielsen hunched up her pretty shoulders when she felt the draft and uttered a little cry that caused several people to look up in surprise; for a few seconds there was silence in the room.[9]

The governor has in effect been told that this meal is the valedictory summing-up of the old days. Shock waves from the shots in Sarajevo have hoisted the curtain into a sail, leave-taking is imminent; the war, the candle flames and death, the worms, trigger a deeply physical reaction in Mrs Nielsen, whose cry is instinctively interpreted by the others as a universal implication.

No matter how secure Otto might still feel, this is also an announcement of *his* death. The fallout from Sarajevo effects everybody, with Otto's fate being one of the consequences. The whys and wherefores of his death are embedded in the Stein family situation and in the overall circumstances of the times. Otto's fate is thus an offshoot of the downward trajectory that engulfs his father. When Thorvald Stein goes outside after the dinner party in order to lower the flag, he finds this national symbol hanging limp and dark against the flagpole; as it comes down, the slack fabric snakes itself around his face. He is suddenly unable to secure the rope: "It's as if I've lost control of my hand",[10] he tells his son Jørgen, who has to take over and complete the procedure. This is the first symptom of the ailment that initially affects the governor's arm, and will eventually claim his life. He is handing over a taxing baton to Jørgen – and thereby also to Otto. Danish literary scholar Marianne Sørensen sums this up with great precision: "Otto is a whited sepulchre, and his eventual suicide is a substantial gauge in the story of the Stein family's decline, of its insufficient capacity for survival in the new age."[11]

Kinships

History repeats itself, would seem to be Jacob Paludan's point when drawing a parallel to a novel by Danish writer

Herman Bang (1857–1912), the title of which he could easily have borrowed for his own book: *Haabløse slægter* (1880; Hopeless Generations). In Bang's novel, the degenerate Ludvig Høg, a public official in Randers, a town in eastern Jutland, and his wife Stella, who has never really grown up, throw a lavish party for the local bigwigs. During the dinner, held in the autumn of 1863, conversation turns to King Frederik VII's illness and the increased risk of war should he die. A telegram announcing the king's death arrives, the guests all stand up with reverential devotion; Ludvig speaks: "'Hard times will come,' said Høg. Stella started extinguishing the candles on the sideboard..."[12] The story then jumps directly to the point in the Second Schleswig War of 1864 when the people of Randers are awaiting invasion by the enemy. While Ludvig is helping the visiting crown prince escape, Stella is looking after their critically ill infant son, who simply suffers from insufficient capacity for survival. He dies at the very moment the crown prince gallops out of the town, all accompanied by this striking window symbolism:

> The window pounded noisily against the wall. The wind grabbed the curtain and worked it loose, so it flapped like a banner far into the room; the flame in the lamp flared up and smoked... [...] The window crashed noisily against the wall, one of the panes shattered, and the shards clattered onto the stone steps.[13]

Thomas Mann's novel *Buddenbrooks: The Decline of a Family* (1901, *Buddenbrooks – Verfall einer Familie*) similarly opens with a detailed description of a grandiose dinner, the inaugural party for the Buddenbrooks' recently acquired house, in which many events of family and business lives will be played out. Even though the grand new house signifies a hitherto glittering highpoint for the family firm, Thomas Mann scatters symptoms of decline across the dinner table. Later on, the Buddenbrooks mark yet another milestone with an even bigger and more beautiful house, their last one, of which the head of the family, Thomas Buddenbrook, says:

> When the house is finished, death follows. […] I know that the external, visible, tangible tokens and symbols of happiness and success first appear only after things have in reality gone into decline already. Such external signs need time to reach us, like the light of one of those stars up there, which when it shines most brightly may well have already gone out, for all we know.[14]

In an essay on Thomas Mann, Jacob Paludan calls *Buddenbrooks* a "typical novel of death, every line points downwards to the perishable and the grave".[15]

Familial motivation

The breeziness and the sense of security in Otto's upbringing underlie his later involvement in an extremely risky business – he can walk on water, can he not. Others cannot imagine the outbreak of war; by the same token, Otto cannot imagine anything getting too hot for *him* to handle. He was born into a golden life, and *that* is an immutable fact.

The apartment into which Otto later moves is more than a match for the governor's residence! The demeaning of his family torments him; he wants to fly the flag again, and so he turns himself into a 'man of the world'. In so doing, he breaks with a family tradition: nothing could persuade him to be a public official like his father. In Otto's opinion, *that* institution is well on its way to becoming obsolete, which is wholly in line with actual developments in Denmark at the time.

There is a wide disparity between Otto's first-rate family pedigree and the meagre financial assistance the family is able to provide while he is a student. He ought to be sitting in fashionable Restaurant Wivel, with a lot of show and rustling of bank notes, but he is not – and this state of affairs has to be rectified, cost what it may. Resources only stretch to the role of onlooker, but Otto wants to be where things are happening. Limited financial support from home is an illustration of how the family situation in general is of no help to an ambitious Otto.

The lost present day

Younger brother Jørgen has great difficulty in leaving the childhood home, and just before the dinner party he tries out an old wooden raft "he had played with as a child"[16] to see if it can still hold him. He poles the raft out into the fjord, but nearly capsizes and is in real danger of drowning. Throughout the novel, Jørgen remains of an intensely regressive disposition; his capacity for self-expression is inhibited, and every day sees him treading water. The water he is attempting to navigate with the raft is referred to as "this unmerciful element",[17] and thus adult life is labelled too.

Jørgen and Otto employ different methods of navigation. Jørgen hangs onto the past; Otto cannot get to the future fast enough; neither has a compass embedded in the present. Their childhood home, which eventually disintegrates, is also a small-scale picture of the irrevocable loss of sanctuary and stability that was brought about by the First World War. The war turns values upside down, should they endure at all, when even the most commonplace modes of expression lose their impact. As the narrator says: "Seen against the background of the war, many of the mind's perspectives that had appeared so impressive now seemed quite limited – it was like looking through the wrong end of a telescope. The blasé tone of voice that people had readily accepted now had a hollow ring, and gestures that had had a hypnotic effect seemed naive."[18]

Everyone is threatened by the unfathomable. Jørgen adrift in the water, which will "smilingly engulf him",[19] is an anticipation of Otto's death. Walking to the wooden raft, Jørgen sees a dead flatfish lying in the harbour basin, "white and motionless as a discarded stiff shirtfront",[20] an ominous projection into a future in which the party comes to a standstill for man-about-town Otto.

Boundless ambition

Otto's eventual fate is a threat to everybody, given that he is the one least expected to end up in such a predicament. He makes for himself – to all outward appearances, that is – a glittering career.

Having passed his law exams, Otto gets a job in the office of respected lawyer Smit. Everything about the place displeases Otto: his title, junior chief clerk, is humiliating; the pay is awful; sitting in a half-heated front office is anything but fun; the tasks he is given, more or less those of a bookkeeper, are deadly dull. Otto seems unduly impatient and demanding. On the other hand, his desire to get on in life is understandable. He will not settle for what is at hand if there is the slightest chance of reaching for something better – which is a both dangerous and sympathetic feature of Otto's character.

He leaves Smit and takes wing in a job with the law firm owned by senior lawyer Goos, who turns out to be an old student friend of his father, Thorvald Stein; Goos receives Otto "like a son"![21]

Otto advances swiftly and is soon entitled to take on his own clients and investments, as long as he pays Goos a fee. It is not long before Otto takes the next step up the ladder and becomes acting head of the firm. Goos, it seems, is busy with all manner of business outside his legal practice; he is even involved with a company selling trout. The activities that prevent him from attending to work at the office are strangely diffuse and suspicious. His absence, on the other hand, allows Otto free rein to indulge in double-dealing, thus betraying Goos' fatherly trust in him. Betrayal goes both ways, however, given that Goos has abandoned his 'son' and left him to his own devices.

The authorities, 'father figures', have their share of responsibility in Otto's fate. Becoming suspicious of Otto's activities, Thorvald Stein turns to Goos, who rejects any misgivings out of hand, praising Otto to the skies. This substantiates the picture of an 'alliance' between Goos and Thorvald Stein. In his reaction here, Goos is effectively acting as a repressive factor in the district governor. This is actually the state of affairs for an entire generation as depicted in the novel. The case of Jørgen's friend Leif Hansen, for example. Leif's boss forsakes him in exactly the same way Goos forsakes Otto. The consequences are disastrous for Leif, who is accused of a fraud committed by another employee in his office while the boss has been absent on shady business. Leif feels sorely tempted to commit the fraud in question himself, and for a while he is also on the verge of committing suicide. It is thus no coincidence that Otto's widow, Lily, falls in love with Leif.

Deceit at the core – Gatsby and Grünlich

Otto's law-breaking, perpetrated inside the office, points up the covert side of the head of the firm's activities outside the office. Jacob Paludan might have had an eye to F. Scott Fitzgerald's novel *The Great Gatsby* (1926), in which criminality behind the façade is a substantial element of the zeitgeist. Otto's sweetest dream must have been of a lavish lifestyle comparable with that of Jay Gatsby. The embodiment of the American dream, Jay Gatsby has built his fortune on bootlegging alcohol, and he is in all probability a kingpin of organised crime.

In Thomas Mann's *Buddenbrooks*, the Buddenbrook firm is the epitome of an impeccable German business culture. And yet a conman, Bendix Grünlich, manages to marry into the Buddenbrook dynasty, where family and firm are inseparable. Grünlich's deceitful dealings have led him way out of his depth, but he manages to reach shore temporarily by means of marriage with Antonie Buddenbrook. Her father, Johann Buddenbrook, is duped by the fraudulent documents that

Grünlich produces as proof of his worthiness to be a son-in-law. Johann Buddenbrook seeks background information from his prospective son-in-law's business associates. They too deceive him because Grünlich owes them large sums of money, which they can only recoup by praising him to his future father-in-law in the hope that their outstanding dues will be covered by the dowry. This is exactly what happens; companies with an equally illustrious reputation as Buddenbrook are not averse to deception: they 'recommend' Grünlich in glowing terms, and Johann Buddenbrook believes that in his son-in-law he has found the brilliant German business brain of the future.

Once married, Grünlich persists with his shady transactions, which he is able to finance by virtue of his creditworthy status as Johann Buddenbrook's son-in-law. When cracks start appearing in the Buddenbrook firm, it becomes impossible for Grünlich to obtain credit. His creditors see him as the cause of the cracks! Grünlich is the corrupt core of the Buddenbrook dynasty – just like Otto is the corrupt core at the heart of *his* setting. Grünlich's fraud is incorporated as an element of the German business culture, given that "it is well known that his business is flourishing, branching out in all directions."[22]

Grünlich eventually has to beg his father-in-law for financial help; Johann Buddenbrook discovers Grünlich's true character and pulls the rug from under his feet. He thinks that by doing so he will have weeded out the root of this particular evil, but Antonie and Bendix Grünlich are now parents to a daughter, Erika, who is a replica of her father! Erika marries a director, Hugo Weinschenk, and he also turns to fraud and ends up in prison.

Weinschenk is the new Grünlich; although the family is far more tolerant of Weinschenk, saying he belongs with the Buddenbrooks despite his guilt. They even hold "Christmas Eve at the Buddenbrooks' with an indicted man in their midst!"[23] The family look upon Weinschenk as a man who "had probably done nothing worse than what most of his colleagues blithely did every day".[24]

According to Christian Buddenbrook: "Seen in the light of day, actually, every businessman is a swindler".[25] Christian is brother to Antonie and to Thomas, the latter taking over the business when Johann Buddenbrook dies. Christian is the flipside of the family coin, the front face of which is adorned with the glittering Thomas. In *Jørgen Stein*, Jørgen is considered to be the black sheep, while everyone believes Otto to be the family's star. In a comparison between *Jørgen Stein* and *Buddenbrooks*, Danish author and literary scholar Niels Barfoed declares Otto's huge consumption of tobacco products to have been inherited from Christian![26]

In 1954, Thomas Mann published his novel *The Confessions of Felix Krull, Confidence Man: The Early Years* (1954, *Bekenntnisse des Hochstaplers Felix Krull. Der Memoiren, erster Teil*), part one of a work that remained unfinished. He had been writing the novel periodically since 1910, and in 1922 an extract was published as a short story. Felix Krull's con tricks involve straightforward theft and swapped identity. By stealing from a wealthy woman he is able to live a double-life, which brings him into contact with a young marquis and his mistress. The marquis' parents intend to send him on a Grand Tour in order to thwart this love affair. Taking on Krull's identity, the marquis is able to stay with his beloved; Krull, in the guise of Marquis Louis Venosta, travels out into the world looking for adventure. All highly entertaining, with aesthetical and identity-psychological subtleties alike, but the swindles committed do not have the same socio-economic significance that we see in *Buddenbrooks*.

Fraternal choices

Otto has to live up to the prevailing view that he has chosen the well-established and steady route, unlike his brother. From their mother's point of view, law is a way to make a living, whereas philosophy, which Jørgen chooses to study, is a hobby. Jørgen nonetheless passes his university exams in philosophy as his principal subject before switching to art history, which never really comes to much more than a feeling of superfluity and detachment from down-to-earth life. Jørgen is convinced that Otto is the lucky one, his life forging ahead as he operates at the centre of events – and, in a sense, that is true!

En route Jørgen also makes a clumsy attempt at writing poems – about glorious days gone by. He has a little more success when he switches from art history to journalism; now he feels as if he has stepped into life proper, but this requires compromise and adjustment. The newspaper for which he writes will not print his controversial articles, and so he makes a drastic change: he gets a job as a filling-station attendant. This new lifestyle proves a little *too* authentic. His regressive tendencies take him back to Havnstrup, where he lives the life of a smallholder and husband, and has the firm intention of concentrating entirely on animals and produce, even setting up a poultry business. He eventually adds an intellectual aspect to this earth-bound existence by making a limited return to his journalism.

Implicit faith

Expectations of Otto are many and sky-high, and he is hell-bent on fulfilling them with not a shadow of doubt that he will go far. The others view him as a promising lawyer; in his own eyes, he is an *exceptionally* promising lawyer. Otto's self-confidence is both charmingly limitless and alarming. On the other hand, it is not until there is real substantiation for suspicion that real alarm sets in.

Otto, *he's* the real deal, everyone thinks; no messing around for him, and, unlike Jørgen, no wasting time on all manner of philosophical thoughts either. Those within Otto's orbit are of the opinion that he knows exactly what he wants. According to his father, Otto is: "a good, able young man to whom the future lay open. Never had he shown any signs of a proclivity for loose living."[27] The implication being that the same cannot be said of Jørgen.

Jørgen sees Otto as his "hitherto superior brother",[28] and their mother points out that Otto cheers up the family: "Isn't it lucky, though, that things are going so well for Otto".[29] Otto is the recipe for a boy-wonder and a shining example for everyone in the novel!

While tragic destiny is overtaking Otto, he is captive to the implicit faith of his surrounding world that he will thrive. This glaring contrast projects an ominous picture of loneliness. No one is taken into his confidence, and even though he has a number of friends he can visit when holidaying at his childhood home, their identities are never revealed. In Copenhagen his friends comprise the 'connections' of whom he likes to brag.

Otto's path to deception is flagged early on in the novel when the family is on its way to the North Sea coast: "Long before they were able to see the sea, the sky gave signs of it."[30] This preparation for what is to come might also apply to Jacob Paludan's elegant construction of the character Otto Stein.

The Otto who piles on the weight while carrying out his deceit started out as a sturdy figure. Just before the dinner party at the beginning of the novel there is mention of how "steady his hand was" and about "his hips, which filled every bit of his trousers".[31] During the dinner, a customs inspector boasts of being the only person present able to eat forty oysters at one sitting; Otto thinks that the voice of youth ought to be heard on the subject and he dives into the food. Similarly, an extreme nicotine habit later becomes a lifebuoy, although Otto is a heavy smoker from the outset.

Otto and the narrator

The other characters in the novel misjudge Otto. In a similarly 'inaccurate' vein the narrator frequently expresses a highly black-and-white view of him: "He was not deeply versed in psychology, but he could tell when things were being carried a little too far", or he was "of a stolid disposition" with an "armorplated skin", which prevents him from undertaking "[a]bstruse speculation about the nature of his own psychological processes".[32] These stereotypical statements give rise to misgivings about the reliability of the narrator. Even reviewers who are most enthusiastic about the depiction of Otto accept the narrator's one-sided interpretations. Danish literary historian Emil Frederiksen (1902–1992), for example, is simply of the opinion that Otto has no "intellectual weight" but, on the contrary, "a pound of stupidity under his brow".[33]

Another Danish literary historian, Søren Schou, is the only analyst to make direct reference to the narrator *and* Otto pairing. According to Søren Schou, the narrator wraps Otto in "false loyalty, which just manages to intimate the underlying sarcasm"; by so doing, the narrator contributes to the exposure of Otto's self-deception.[34] From time to time "the kid glove is pulled from the iron fist" and the narrator gets stuck in like a "particularly straightforward satirist".[35] In other words, Søren Schou considers Otto to be answerable to the narrator, to be his 'victim'.

When digging deeply into Otto's story, as in the case of this study, the circumscribed role played by the narrator leaps from the page. The narrator has a restricted view, which does not allow for the possibility of fathoming Otto's depths. Otto is bigger than the narrator. He has enough psychological sense to conduct a lengthy bout of whip-cracking at the targets in his conman's circus ring, while also duping the narrator!

In Dostoevsky's fictional world, the narrator might well describe a character in a highly one-dimensional fashion, and that character might then suddenly flex an independent muscle and display a surprising spectrum of light and shade. This resembles, in my opinion, the way in which Otto wriggles out of his narrator's clinch. It is highly probable that Jacob Paludan has taken a leaf out of Dostoevsky's book by employing his stratagem of letting a narrator with a restricted horizon inject the fictional universe with a broader dynamic range.[36]

Any sympathy the reader feels for Otto can be accounted for by this one-sidedness in his depiction by the narrator. Despite his criminal deeds, we come to his defence. Dostoevsky is the absolute master of engendering sympathy for the criminal, and this sympathy is often proportional to the crime.

I would claim that Otto has quite a portion of Russian blood coursing through his veins; Dostoevsky exercised considerable influence on Jacob Paludan. In the following passage from an essay about Dostoevsky, Jacob Paludan highlights a common ground with the Russian in matters of the inscrutable mind:

> Since he knew vice as a reality, and not just as a demanding desk job, he has the privilege that, in him, less virtuous readers sense someone who knows them [...] Dostoevsky is for those who have felt, like Goethe, the seed of everything imaginable within themselves, not for the utterly spotless and dustless suit and tie.[37]

Angel from the past

Three women play a role in Otto's short life: Lily, his wife, a woman of great complexity; his mistress Wanda; spontaneous Eva, the one who got away, the young woman from his past.

While Otto's marriage is grinding to a halt, and he is up to his neck in fraud, one day his car breaks down on a country road in north Zealand, giving him a sorely needed breathing space. He is close to the farm called Brogaard where he had first met Eva years ago, and he wonders if everything would have been different if he had chosen that happy young woman, who had openly shown her attraction to him. The paradisiacal Eva was lively and vigorous, as full of fun as a kitten. She was 'musical', and was indeed studying to be an organist. In Eva, Otto had an unpretentious and abject admirer who would have been more than content with the landscape as it was.

Eva struck a most seductive chord, but Otto sidestepped the proposition, which was the right call for him. His ambitions lead him to ruin, but he would have sunk even faster with Eva, who would have been the option of a comfortable, but soporific, life devoid of opportunity to follow his ambitions. More fundamentally, she represents innocence, which a striving man would find it impossible to preserve, and she is the idyll of the past from which someone who operates purely in forward gear must withdraw.

The Brogaard farm belonged to Eva's uncle, and he had taken the young people for a drive in his car. First the uncle, Mr Hambro, stops at a temperance café, which, many years later, will be the setting for Otto's final cup of coffee, and then he wants to show them a marsh pool:

> "Let's not walk too far," Otto begged when Hr. Hambro led them a short distance into the woods to show them the waterhole, all that remained of an old marl pit. It was a small, quiet, isolated lake bordered by a wall of spruces and birches whose gossamer foliage stood out in sharp contrast to the somber atmosphere of the place. Silently they looked out over the water which seemed to have absorbed the darkness of all the previous winter's nights and to be hiding it for the rest of the summer.
> "Ugh!" said Eva suddenly.
> Otto shifted his melancholy gaze from the lake and looked at her.[38]

Otto is reluctant because it is the very same marsh pool into which he will one day sink one step before intended, and he is not the only one to sense this; Eva, too, feels the chill of death enveloping Otto: "Ugh!" The marsh pool with its perpetual darkness awaits him. Perhaps he turns his gaze from the water to Eva in the hope of rescue, but the trajectory links her to the darkness of the deep, and he is fundamentally acknowledging that he would also go under if they were together.

Princess of poverty

Once married, Otto would not dream of cheating on his wife, but before meeting Lily he keeps a mistress, Wanda Bauer. He is also the fantasist conjuring up his own narrative – but that requires capital. Wanda is Austrian, a stage performer, and when waiting for her outside the theatre Otto thinks himself very much the European man-about-town. There is an international aura to the affair; Wanda could have stepped from the page in one of the French novels that are Otto's favourite reading.

With his literary castles in the air, Otto is not bothered that Wanda is actually a 'chorus girl' performing at the revue theatre. He sees this as risqué, just like her address; she lives in one of the poorest neighbourhoods of Copenhagen. Romanticising Wanda's home is also a way of making his visits to the area tolerable. Sight of the backyards casts the die both for Otto's frauds and for his suicide: anything but poverty. The thought of ending in poverty is so abhorrent to Otto that high stakes and death are preferable.

Nonetheless, conducting a relationship with Wanda ushers Otto into the realm of poverty. She informs him that their happy-go-lucky lovemaking has borne fruit: he is going to be a father. This triggers his first act of deception. There is absolutely no way that Otto will even contemplate paying for the maintenance of mother and child by cutting down on his personal consumption and expenditure. Holding back now, at the best time in a young life, was simply not an option but a foretaste of death, he reasons; and thus he has embarked upon his race against death.

Otto's deceit gets underway the moment he becomes a father – again coupling 'paternal authority' and fraud. Were that not enough, Otto becomes a father *as a result of* deceit: the maintenance Wanda extorts from him should rightly have been paid by another man. Otto deceives because of his desire for unrestricted consumption rather than any paternal feelings; but he is not actually the father anyway. This becomes clear when his wife Lily sees the three-year-old child in the street; spotting absolutely no resemblance whatsoever to his supposed father, she utterly rejects the claim that the boy is Otto's son.

Wanda does not settle for the initial maintenance sum, but gradually increases her financial demands, becoming the very image of poverty eating its way into the increasingly wealthy (on paper) Otto. Wanda mirrors Otto, highlighting the universality of deceit. She does to Otto what he does to others. Hard-up Wanda cheats wealthy Otto; although, in reality, he is the hard-up man cheating the wealthy.

The father-son theme is age-old and ever-present. In the modernist context of *Ulysses* (1922), James Joyce depicts the rootlessness of this juxtaposition: "if the father who has not a son be not a father can the son who has not a father be a son?"[39] Otto's father figures leave him without wealth, and what does the future hold for Otto's son who is not his son?

Otto's queen

Lily is Otto's dream woman; a beauty, light as thistledown, his physical opposite. She is "the slender Lily", dresses cling to her "like the fragile and fragrant petals of a flower".[40] Even her breath is fragrant, given her considerable appetite for lozenges. Nor is it a drawback, from Otto's point of view, that she is always expensively dressed and the centre of attention wherever she goes. For a man who firmly intends to be a majestic presence in the world, Lily is the perfect queen.

Otto's taste in novels is again a factor: Lily is the prototype of the young woman with the wealthy father. Her particular father has a professor title and attributes his wealth to big business deals and his notable inventions. Otto sees Lily as a combination of beauty and money; she is "a lovely lady whose father went hurtling like an economic high-explosive shell from one country to another, his brief case stuffed with patents."[41] The professor has taken Lily along on his many trips abroad, and she conducts herself like an overindulged woman-of-the-world, which is fine with Otto because not for a second does he doubt that he can provide her with the same level of extravagance.

Nor does Lily doubt that he can. She tells Jørgen that making money is the most important thing in this world, and he responds that Otto is as good as gold. She informs Otto quite bluntly that a husband must be able to give her everything. Otto is impeccable in the role of perfect candidate, and his most lucrative deceit is executed just before he makes her an offer of marriage.

Lily is convinced that Otto will be an even better sponsor for a carefree existence than her father has been. In this she is mistaken – and yet not. Marriage with Otto does indeed extend her happy-go-lucky lifestyle, given that her father dies shortly after the wedding, heavily in debt. Otto, who had been expecting a hefty inheritance from the professor, is shaken to his core. Just how surprised Lily might be remains ambiguous. Perhaps the shock does not strike home until later when she discovers that Otto is a charlatan, just like her father.

The professor's estate contained no patent rights, and his real line of business turns out to have been currency speculation, which reaped heavy losses. What is more, he had been a frequent guest at various casinos, and he had a fondness, as Lily well knew, for 'high stakes'. Cause of death cannot be determined, but nor can it be ruled out that, via suicide, the professor has mapped a route for his son-in-law.

The 'professor' title was apparently conferred abroad, inferring that it is fake. Despite a phoney title and imaginary patent rights, Lily's father *had* actually come up with some inventions. They are even attributed particular topicality after the outbreak of war, coming under the 'chemical' category. So saying, the father's 'phony professor' title is spot on: it fits all those professors responsible for chemical warfare. Jacob Paludan is always merciless in his critique of war and all its works. Lily's father also represents those for whom the First World War was simply an extra business opportunity.

Lily is another example of someone whose 'origins' leave them without financial means. In her case this is reinforced by a general lack of knowledge about her mother. Lily is not just the lovely young woman let down by father and husband alike, two men with striking similarities. That Otto chooses to be involved with her specifically is also a reflection of his life without a safety net: Lily is descended from a fantasist of a father, who is a speculator and professor of castles in the air, and from a mother whose identity is pure guesswork. Otto marries into a picture of the life he has constructed upon foundations of imagination and risky business.

Nor is Lily exactly an angel herself. She is an inveterate flirt; that the flirting never reaches consummation is not due to any reticence on her part but to inhibitions in her victims. She is characterised by a mixture of ingenuousness and know-how: "There was something indefinable and exotic about her. Often she seemed like a slightly overage flapper, but under certain circumstances her face and features would reflect real maturity and boundless experience."[42] Lily's two-timing disposition bears the hallmark of universality, hence she cannot be held responsible.

Lily and Otto live stylishly, with all manner of consumer goods, an expensive car and the most modern and fashionable apartment in Copenhagen. Even so, their marriage swiftly breaks down and they are soon living in two separate worlds. Otto still has to deal with the bills pouring in from Lily's non-stop shopping and participation in a frenetic nightlife.

Eventually, Otto only sees Lily when she pops home in the morning to get some sleep, which Danish literary historians Martin Zerlang and Henrik Reinvaldt interpret thus: "The expansion of nightlife entertainment (bars, cinemas, nightclubs, and so forth), brought about by the increase in production during the 1920s, moves sexuality out of the sphere of intimacy. This development [...] is particularly thematised in the relationship between Otto and Lily."[43] Danish critic and dramatist Henning Kehler (1891–1979) has a pithy comment to the couple's life outside the intimate sphere: "If you have lived in Denmark and Copenhagen, then you have met Otto Stein and his wife Lily."[44]

A decisive change in Lily's feelings occurs when Otto desperately attempts to turn the fiscal tide by buying racehorses. The horses fail to win, and Lily has a glacial sense of the loser in her husband. It is a painful picture, in which the outcome on a trotting track proves to be the epitaph over all Otto's ventures.

Despite their substantial marital difficulties there is a sense of strong feelings, also on Lily's part, Otto's most treasured possession. Shortly before his suicide, he wonders if he will ever see her again. Perhaps he would have turned around had he believed there was anything to be salvaged.

The future as guarantor

While still a law student, Otto thinks he should already be afforded the opportunities and the income available to fully-qualified lawyers; it is unjust that he, of all people, should be kept away from the action. Patience is not one of his virtues. Once he is a qualified lawyer, he keeps a constant eye on the next step up, the career advancement he deserves – and so on. Otto starts using financial fraud as a way to redress the incongruity that he is not yet in possession of the capital to which he is entitled and will acquire: "What a damned shame it was that a person could not thrust his hand forth into the assured abundance of the future and scrape back into the penurious present a supply of ready cash!"[45]

Jacob Paludan's portrait of Otto also illustrates a rebellion on behalf of youth in general. Otto is a young person's Robin

Hood, as is implied by Leif and their common destiny: "Why should we young people go hungry while the older folks are stuffing themselves? We have to break through such prejudices, and somebody has to lead the way."[46]

Otto feels he was made for the roaring '20s. He is in no doubt whatsoever that he has a stake in the golden calf, and he lives his life accordingly. Fancy meals in elegant restaurants are therefore a daily requirement. The food must be accompanied by drinks of the highest quality, but Otto never becomes inebriated; style is important and self-control essential.

Status symbols are of great importance to Otto, and he even achieves mention in the tabloid press of the day. He uses status symbols as a barometer of success. It could almost be said that if Otto goes by the book, moving in the 'right' places with the 'right' people, then he considers himself blameless. He never actually gets to a state of feeling real guilt. There is something both psychopathic and touchingly childlike about Otto; not an uncommon combination. The eponymous protagonist of *The Great Gatsby* also follows this recipe; not a trace of guilty conscience in him either. Originally named James Gatz, he calls himself Jay Gatsby and "to this conception he was faithful to the end"; he sees himself as someone who is simply serving higher powers in his "instinct toward his future glory".[47]

The price of generosity

Otto derives great pleasure from all that is fine and refined, and he is also motivated by satisfying his aesthetic sense. In addition, he has an intense desire to share this delight with others, rolling out all the bonhomie and charm that personify the perfect host. Otto's generous nature requires serious funding. He "should presumably be able to step up to any table and stand drinks all around without having anything as debasing as consideration of cost stay a hand so naturally inclined toward the broad gesture."[48]

Money sits very loosely in Otto's pocket; he takes every opportunity to spread a little happiness. The kiosk assistant, the waiters and drivers, all receive generous tips, satisfying Otto's perpetual need for attention and appreciation. His criminal actions, which fund this munificence, do not preclude the novel from deploying his profligacy as a positive counter-image to savings accounts and puritanism.

Big spender

'Money makes the world go around' is Otto's simple philosophy, and money makes his world spin faster and faster. His short life thus highlights his belief that *money* "decided things in the world today, not age".[49] Live lavishly, die young. Otto sees profit as the end that justifies all means. Cheat or be cheated. The provenance of the banknotes is immaterial, money is not dirty, ideals are but packaging; Otto thinks he is simply living in accordance with "this age-old wisdom", as Emil Frederiksen puts it.[50]

Otto's profligacy, in which he loses himself, is also a macabre illustration of another view he holds of 'economics', of life as "the cruel, relentless world of business that asks nothing of the fates, is indifferent to happiness and life and death itself, and has only one objective – the turnover of commodities."[51] To this Martin Zerlang and Henrik Reinvaldt add the angle that Otto's death can also be read as the loss of 'self': "His suicide […] is the definitive corroboration that he has drowned his personality in the waters of turnover."[52]

The innocent conman

A wealthy dentist has died; having no heir, he has left his entire estate to foundations and non-profit organisations. Otto handles the will, the accounts for the foundations and the monies owing through unpaid bills. After the estate has been wound up, one item of debt remains outstanding but written-off as uncollectible. Otto just so happens to hear that the debtor does actually have the funds to pay the balance due. He calls in the 400 kroner[53] owing, but then 'forgets' to pay it into the foundation account. Initially, he sees this oversight as being "a circumstance that was not surprising in a big, busy office", and he later calls it a "working loan"[54] that he tells himself he will repay.

'Unsurprising circumstance' and 'working loan' are Otto's justification for what turns out to be his first act of fraud. He actually seems to believe in this version of his personal conduct. Although Otto might find the complications caused by this and subsequent frauds highly irritating, there is no sense of self-criticism. On the contrary, his irritation is an expression of anger against those people whose money he has appropriated for himself. Otto takes the stance that calling him to account is unjust and petty-minded. He is not the criminal – no, the other party is the offender, and sometimes Otto even has the temerity to let fly at this 'wrongdoer'.

Jacob Paludan presents a fascinating psychological profile of the criminal, also with regard to the consequences for the offender. The second after he has committed his first act of fraud, Otto's high spirits desert him for ever, not because of a bad conscience, but because he can already feel pursuers breathing down his neck.

The guilty client

Otto's single largest act of fraud involves Arthur Klein, a naïve young man who inherits his wealthy father's estate. Otto strikes instinctively, a predator: "Otto smelled an estate."[55]

He is quick to convince Klein that the best course of action would be to invest 70,000 kroner[56] in a third mortgage bond on a property in a Copenhagen suburb. That is the face value of the mortgage deed, but it could actually be bought for just 30,000 kroner, and after various 'expenses' Otto would pick up 35,000 kroner. What is more, the entirety of the father's estate had been valued at 140,000 kroner, and Otto, who gives himself credit for not having taken the whole sum all at once, uses the remaining 70,000 kroner as a bank from which he gradually withdraws funds.

The story is also about the past catching up with you. The Klein-transactions are the first to eat away at Otto Stein, and contribute most potently to his eventual downfall. It is no accident that we have the constellation Stein-Klein, which is also a miniature depiction of the methods Otto employs on his prey and the substantial role their naivety plays in 'the blame'.

Otto capitalises on Klein's delicate state of grief – or simulation of the same – over his father's death. The mortgage bond is also one that is simply crying out for "some worthy idiot".[57] Otto has chosen a document that looks just as trustworthy as he does: eight folio pages covered with the finest legal Latin and equipped with a profusion of impressive signatures, the names of departmental top dogs, lawyers, and so forth. Klein falls hook, line and sinker for this impressive deed, while pretending to understand the wording so as not to lose face – as Otto has of course anticipated. Otto also rushes his client: buy now, the bond is in great demand, and Klein is not going to be the man to hang back.

Otto plays the consummate illusionist – and enjoys the role. He more or less convinces himself that he is helping an unfortunate inexperienced fatherless young man move on in the world. The description of Otto's transaction with Klein is quick-witted and has moments of great humour. Having liberated the 70,000 kroner by selling bonds from the estate, Otto accompanies Klein to the bank in order to deposit the cash, where it will stay until purchase of the mortgage bond the following day. Klein is entirely duped by Otto's scheme:

> With hands that trembled a little he counted out the hundred and forty 500-krone notes at the bank teller's window – fourteen bundles with ten notes in each. The eyes of both bank clerks and customers were on him, and he took care to sound unconcerned:

"And now we'll deposit it in an account until tomorrow."
What extravagance, Klein thought, overwhelmed. Setting up a bank account for only one day! Why, it had taken his father years to wear out a single passbook.[58]

What has taken the father years, Otto will achieve in no time at all. After the show at the bank, Otto gets Klein firmly on the hook by charging only the lowest standard fee for his services and then inviting the young man out to lunch! An outstanding scene. After lunch, which Klein insists on paying for, Otto takes him to view the property. In the taxi an inebriated Klein sings "snatches of funeral hymns and an exceedingly old music-hall hit". Otto does not show his client the actual and somewhat shabby property in which the young man has just invested, but points out a handsome and imposing building, even taking him into the entrance hall: "First-rate, what? And good, solid tenants." Flaunting the 'fine house' instead of the realities is also an amusing reminder of how Otto presents himself – and indeed of how he sees himself; once the target has swallowed the bait, he reflects: "Yes, he was a financier, all right".[59]

Full-blown swindle

It is said of Otto that he "wanted to be right in the middle of the stream of prosperity, and he intended to dig some ingenious side-channels for it when it showed signs of shifting its course."[60] Otto manages to bleed many clients of their capital before he drowns in it. He has hooked some big fish, but even the secretary and student assistant at his own office 'entrust' their money to him, and he gets his hands on the money his brother's good friend, hard-up Leif, has saved through hard work to pay for singing lessons. His deception strikes far and wide across the social spectrum.

Otto sees fraud as a dangerous game in the spirit of the times, a zeitgeist that matches up to eternal truths: life is a game of high odds, and you must dare to gamble. To get the best out of life, live dangerously. We all live on the brink of the abyss, so you might as well dance on it – which is what Otto ends up doing. There is no end to the many irons that have to go into the fire to keep the circus going. He is constantly juggling money in order to keep his con tricks under wraps:

> Indeed, things sometimes went as they did with magicians – suddenly there was nothing under the top hat, then just as suddenly something would appear there. It was simply a question of Otto himself standing over the hat all the time and with the magician's wand directing the vagrant sums of money so that they were always there whenever a forehead began to show wrinkles of anxiety.[61]

The more the wand waves, the more Otto obsesses about the big deal, the "skyscraper deals"[62] that will make it all add up in a peaceful unified whole – the transaction of which Grünlich in *Buddenbrooks* and undoubtedly every tormented big-time swindler dreams. This is not how it turns out, neither for Grünlich nor for Otto. Whenever monies owing are due, it all eventually gets too hot: "Otto was dancing on eggs."[63]

Of Otto's story, the Danish businessman Preben Erik Nielsen writes: "it is a real 'gambler story' about a man who is willing to risk everything in the casino-economy of the 1920s." He draws a parallel with Dostoevsky's novel *The Gambler* (1866): "Many will remember Dostoevsky's harrowing short novel about the roulette player who stakes his soul in an endless tussle with the wheel and little ball, only to end up a desperate man prepared to go the whole way for his grand idea – the idea of an ultimate system that will eliminate all elements of chance, break the bank and, of course, result in the biggest of payouts."[64] Preben Erik Nielsen points out that inspiration for *The Gambler* came from Dostoevsky's own ludomania, and he quotes Anna Dostoevsky for this characterisation of her husband: "But I soon understood that this was not a simple weakness of will but an all-consuming passion, an elemental force against which even a strong character could not struggle."[65] Preben Erik Nielsen is also going the whole way: Dostoevsky as inspiration for Otto – elegant!

Jacob Paludan himself evidently wanted to direct attention to *The Gambler*, given that it must be the novel referred to here: "'On my honor,' said Jørgen soberly. The tobacco smoke and the lamplight reminded him of a Russian novel in which desperate but high-spirited characters stood around a roulette table."[66]

To Preben Erik Nielsen's comments about *The Gambler*, I would like to add that Dostoevsky's novel is a study in the nature of greed and the abyss to which greed can lead. Despite countless warning signals, the protagonist Alexei already feels like a wealthy man *before* each session at the gaming table, and he ends up completely possessed by 'the roulette'. Passion for gambling is interwoven with sexual passion in a symbolic web; and the setting, Roulettenburg, is a miniature version of the 'gambling culture' of the outside world. Fraud as such is not the theme of the novel, given that the roulette tables are in a public space for all to see and the many deceitful characters and thieves who feature in the story rake in their gains quite openly – the openness being a point in itself.

The screw tightens

The number of delaying options steadily declines, and the end-play sets in when Otto is presented with a demand for monies owing of 3,000 kroner to be paid immediately. Erik Orth, the lawyer acting on behalf of Otto's client, has ensured that if he does not pay up he will have to appear before the council of the bar association. Otto even manages to win a little breathing space in this predicament. At his very moment of need, his boss, Goos, gives him a sum of money to be deposited in the company account. Otto procures a receipt at the bank – along with a crossed cheque for the sum he owes.

He hands over the latter, with profound contempt, to Orth; thanks to judicious timing, Orth cannot present the cheque until the following day and so until such time Otto has the sum at his disposal. This case sums up the nature of the fraud in a nutshell: both Orth and Otto have money, and yet they have no money. Otto is yet again one step ahead, but what will he do if and when the money disappears from the account: "Of course, if it did, all hell would break loose in the morning, but where would he be then? [...] there was still time for consideration."[67]

Advocate of darkness

Erik Orth does not make his approach on behalf of one client alone; he takes on the responsibility as lawyer for everyone to whom Otto owes money.

Goos owns the entire building in which his law firms has its offices; it is very well-maintained, with a particularly sunny view from Otto's window. He can see across to a colleague, where circumstances would seem to be totally different:

> From the south windows, a short distance down the street, could be seen another law office, that of Hr. Toller. But here there was no fresh paint and no vines creeping up the outer wall. The windows were coated with dust, and inside a perpetual semidarkness must reign. When Otto looked over there he felt that things had indeed turned out well, and he considered himself lucky.[68]

It turns out that the semidarkness is Orth's workplace. Jacob Paludan leads our thoughts to Hans Christian Andersen's story "The Shadow" (1847, "Skyggen"), in which the shadow of a scholarly man leaves the sunny side and crawls into the darkness of a house across the street, where provocative truths about life in the light lay hidden. Orth is Otto's shadow, he is the result of the dark regions of Otto's activities – hence the constellation Orth–Otto.

Orth emerges slowly. First he is concealed in the semidarkness, then Otto can just glimpse his nose – it is hideous, as is everything about Orth. There they stand, Otto and Orth, watching one another talk on their respective telephones. They move on to watching while talking with one another on their respective telephones. Otto then visits Orth in his office, whence he can look across to his own office. Eventually, Orth starts to invade Otto's office. This trajectory describes how darkness eats its way into Otto, a man who has gambled everything on achieving a bright and happy life.

Otto frequently thinks he has appeased Orth, whereupon Orth simply turns up with increasingly stiff demands, but it is Otto himself who 'feeds' Orth with the snowballing frauds.

Naturally, Otto is only capable of viewing Orth as a crook. He calls him "a devil – a regular spider", while Orth imagines Otto to be a big "sugar-hungry blowfly".[69] Otto's voracious appetite renders it a given that sooner or later he will fly straight into Orth's web. This juxtaposition triggers thoughts of the relationship between the double-murderer Raskolnikov and the examining magistrate Porfiry Petrovich in Dostoevsky's *Crime and Punishment* (1866). Raskolnikov has long evaded arrest, but Porfiry Petrovich lectures him about the power he holds over the offender:

> Let him do it, let him walk about for a while, I don't mind; I know very well that he's my quarry, and he won't get away from me. Where could he run away to? Abroad, perhaps? [...] The reason he won't escape from me isn't just that there's nowhere to escape to: he can't escape from me *psychologically*, heh-heh! [...] Have you ever seen a moth near a flame? Well, he'll be constantly fluttering around me, all the time, like the moth by the flame [...] And he'll keep circling and circling around me, getting closer and closer every time, – until – snap! He'll fly straight into my jaws, and I'll swallow him down [...].[70]

Porfiry Petrovich tells Raskolnikov several times that he finds his case extremely interesting, and Raskolnikov comes to the chilling awareness that the examining magistrate knows everything. Orth's know-how and manner are highly suggestive of this magistrate. When Otto makes ironic comments about Orth's interest in his activities, for example, Orth retorts: "Good heavens, my dear colleague, how can anyone fail to be interested in such an engaging and well-known man about town – psychologically and in many other respects." In so saying, Orth also stresses Otto's universality. Orth represents the consequences of Otto's actions, right down to a prediction of the tragic ending, saying: "[...] won't you have a smoke? Tobacco calms the nerves; one can almost forget tomorrow over a good cigar. Ah yes – tomorrow."[71]

There is another and more particular motive for Erik Orth's campaign against Otto: revenge for the degradation to which he was subjected when he and Jørgen stayed at the same lodgings in Aalborg, where they were both attending upper secondary school. The landlord and landlady of the lodging house gave preferential treatment to Jørgen, the son of a district governor, at the expense of Erik, the son of a schoolmaster; their daughter, Nanna, who idolised Jørgen, was equally dismissive of Erik, while he in turn was madly in love with her. The accumulated resentment over this social and sexual slight, in which Jørgen sometimes directly participated, and to which Erik was extremely sensitive, is now directed at older brother Otto.[72]

Destructiveness and joie de vivre

Jacob Paludan's portrait of Otto is an immensely detailed description of the way in which someone comes apart psychologically, step by step but without at any point losing the desire for life. It is a virtuoso psychological portrait – and a psychological cliff-hanger. The Otto-figure mixes a highly (self-)destructive element with an immense joie de vivre. We are taken to the very core of an intensely labile character, and when his spectacular free fall comes to an end, the spark also goes out of the novel.

In the entrance hall of his home, Otto has what is called a Bornholm clock – a grandfather clock from the Danish island of Bornholm – to which he is increasingly drawn. The clock is white, the colour of death, and it occurs to Otto that he can stop the march of time by placing the clock's heavy weights in his pockets and jumping into the sea – with gallows humour he imagines that he will jump overboard from the ferry to Bornholm. He nonetheless wants to keep himself intact for as long as possible, because the thought of jumping in close to the propeller fills him with revulsion – hell, no! he thinks. Perhaps the would-be suicide has difficulty facing up to the reality of death. Otto wonders if he would still be conscious when he reached the bottom. His curiosity never leaves him, here expressed as a mental picture of himself bouncing like a ball along the seabed, and he considers calling a newspaper to ask about the depth of the sea.

Otto's speculations about suicide are always succeeded by renewed appetite for life and a profusion of ideas for its continuation. In this context, Otto's evolution is accompanied by multi-layered food symbolism, culminating in the atrociously obese character who walks into the marsh pool.

He initially puts away a volume of food and drink corresponding to the volume of his desired income: "Otto was putting on weight. It was as if his body was discounting in advance the affluence at which he aimed."[73] He grows as fat as the wallet he craves. Once he has defrauded his way to affluence, and is keeping the game in play, he eats like a horse if a venture fails – to console himself and to put back on what he has lost! His appetite reaches its most disturbing levels when the writing is on the wall; then he gorges for the entirety of the life that is in the process of expiring, and he is macabrely said to have swollen up like a white maggot. Food eventually features as Otto's last remaining and positive pleasure in life: even when he is hunted quarry, he still thinks about finding a restaurant, where no one knows him, so he can forget his troubles over a cold and fatty salmon.

The food symbolism is multi-facetted, following a 'process'. The literary reviewers who refer to Otto's obesity put the matter into simplified focus. Danish literary historian Orla Lundbo (1909–1986) sees Otto's weight as a manifestation of his "greedy materialism".[74] Another Danish literary historian, Ib Bondebjerg, pulls no punches when designating Otto "a fat and bloated symbol of the unhealthy, speculative capitalism".[75]

Søren Schou sees the obesity as a symbol of dehumanisation, given that Otto "transforms into a mountain of flesh with few human features left intact", applying the interesting perspective that the story of Otto "tells of a world in the process of destroying all human nature".[76]

Martin Zerlang and Henrik Reinvaldt present an intriguing yet possibly somewhat far-fetched interpretation: in the "excessive gluttony" they see an "incestuous regression", in which Otto wants to "procure maternal solicitude in an oral context".[77] It cannot, of course, be denied out of hand that there are elements of this in the novel, but it comes nowhere close to being an 'issue'. The more relevant factor would be that Otto also comfort eats because of his failed relationship with Lily.

Otto thinks of disappearing to Sweden, but he represents a Danish and West European state of affairs that cannot be resolved by the getaway of just one single individual. Furthermore, he is trapped by symptoms of affluence and overconsumption: diabetes and heartburn. Otto's gambling with money matches his gambling with his health, and in neither case does he hold back; bodily and monetary options are exhausted at one and the same time. A man in an advanced stage of diabetes could not drag himself around abroad, he reasons, and is equally firm in rejecting the drastic dietary changes prescribed by his doctor – cutting down would remove his very raison d'être. The heartburn shows Otto to be caught in his own web, and the boomerang has seared into his very heart: "But lavish eating brings on heartburn. All morning long it is as if a cupping glass has attached itself to the abdomen. The saliva has a sour taste, and one feels as if he wouldn't mind throwing up. But it helps as soon as he begins to fill up again."[78] The vicious spiral is also illustrated through his consumption of tobacco. He eventually reaches the chain-smoking stage; the nicotine could kill him, but death would be instantaneous if he abandoned the cigarettes.

Around the clock

As time passes Otto has to work continually, even at night, in order to protect himself. His *Buddenbrooks* colleague, the conman Grünlich, says: "My very existence is one of unceasing activity."[79] *Jørgen Stein* also parodies a culture that has a high opinion of work for the sake of work. Matters of work gradually fill every corner of Otto's mind; even when he does spare a moment to dream, the telephones carry on ringing. He manages to find some respite in the darkness of the cinema and the calm of the silent films, but he nurtures a constant and nagging fear that rumours of the talking pictures might become reality.

Reading Herman Bang's novel *Stuk* (1887; Stucco), Jacob Paludan would have seen two conmen with their day-and-night work cut out as they feverishly contact all manner of people in an attempt to raise the capital needed to conceal a financial hole that is growing so large it will reveal their deceit. The fraudsters, Spenner and Adolf, leading lights at Victoria-Theatret (the Victoria Theatre), have procured both "the stolen and the counterfeit coin"[80] as start-up and working capital. They are adamant to the very end that everything will turn out fine; they are able to repress the realities by, for example, blaming everyone else – and dining on slap-up meals!

Adolf has raised some of the capital by begging his way to his mother's savings and by signing bills of exchange in his father's name, and upon reaching a state of final desperation – "Every day called upon escape routes"[81] – he squeezes out the last drops of familial blood by pawning his parents' silver. Herman Bang paints an extremely intense picture of Adolf removing the cloth-wrapped silverware from a cupboard in his parents' dining room, bundle by bundle by bundle, and then putting the packages back – now filled with paper! Every night thereafter, Adolf, who lives with his parents, returns home shaking with anxiety until he has run his hand over the bundles and made sure the 'bluff' is still in place. He feels as if he has been given another respite. The paper-filled packages in his parents' cupboard are a condensed manifestation of Adolf's con tricks.

In *Stuk*, too, the deceptions have a universal application: life at the Victoria Theatre becomes a condensed picture of life in the big city, which in turn is a picture of *life* in modern Denmark as a whole: "There aren't any provinces now [...] It's all just one single big Copenhagen . . ."[82] In Herman Bang's picture of this life, the final word is given to privy councillor Hein, who personifies big business in Denmark. Hein has strong suspicions about financial fraud at the theatre, but he waits calmly and quietly in the wings until the time comes to enter and skim the cream off the bankruptcy, which is but a fresh impetus for him. The 'theatre' rises from its ashes with an injection of Hein's capital.

Self-preservation and self-image

Reading about Otto's final days is like watching a fighter jet nosedive from a great height after the pilot loses control. The greater the speed and roar, the more doomed the prospects. The closer to death, the more intense the battle in the cockpit – and, all the while, a hope that the plane will level off. Towards the end, Otto is utterly exhausted and constantly on the go. He is getting so little sleep that real events seem to be happening in a dream. The more he is forced to concentrate on what is close at hand, the more his mind wanders. He has to carry conviction in order to survive, but he can no longer look people in the eye, and he starts repeating himself.

"His brain has been ticking hard day and night for years, and the second hand is accelerating its count-down to zero,"[83] as Preben Erik Nielsen writes of Otto. Even so, Otto remains convinced to the very end that there is still time for deliberation. His sense of loneliness takes on colossal proportions, with an offshoot of paranoia when he suddenly starts thinking that people are touching him from behind. One moment Otto realises that he has been reduced to nothing but an instinct for self-preservation, and the next moment he sweeps such thoughts under the table as nothing but his imagination playing up. Although a natural defence mechanism, this response also kicks-in largely because Otto has never lost his self-image. Orla Lundbo characterises Otto as "self-pitying",[84] but that is precisely what he is *not*. No matter how thin the ice gets, Otto hangs onto his motivating force: "he could not give up the picture of himself as a person richly endowed with talent."[85]

The mask drops

With a wave of his magic wand, Otto had managed to channel 3,000 kroner from Goos to Erik Orth, thereby avoiding, for the time being, an appearance before the council of the bar association, which would have caused his house of cards to collapse. This turns out to be his final wave of the magic wand. Orth can now really smell blood. When he next visits Otto it is in the role of lawyer for Arthur Klein, Otto's main 'sponsor' – Orth has now crawled right under Otto's skin. Orth has been appointed because Klein has tried and tried in vain to get in touch with Otto in order to turn a security into cash and to hear why the tax authorities continue to demand payment of a sum that Otto should have remitted on his behalf. Orth is in no mood to be talked round; on the contrary, he uses the opportunity to request a rundown of all Klein's financial assets – which Otto has long since spent. The game is up. Otto manages to defer inspection of the financial documents until the following day, whereupon he takes flight; he does so with a degree of ambivalence, and to the very end he is tempted to return – to life. But the hopelessness of his situation and his dread of the machinery of justice have mapped out the route to the marsh pool.

King and bull

That the route leads straight into the marsh waters is essentially due to Jacob Paludan's stylistic command over proceedings: he does not vacillate. His steady grip imbues the portrait of Otto with the inexorable power of tragedy as defined in Karen Blixen's story "The Deluge at Norderney" from *Seven Gothic Tales* (1934); when talking about bullfighting, a cardinal outlines two ways of looking at the 'challenge':

> 'It is a picturesque thing,' said the Cardinal. 'And what do you imagine, Madame, that the bull thinks of it? The plebeian bull may well think: "God have mercy on me, what terrible conditions here. What disasters, what a run of bad luck. But it must be endured." And he would be deeply thankful, moved even to humble tears, were the king, in the midst of the bullfight, to send directions to have it stopped, out of compassion for him. But the pure-bred fighting bull falls in with it, and says: "Lo, this is a bullfight." He will have his blood up straight away, and he will fight and die, because otherwise there would be no bullfight out of the thing at all.'[86]

A true bullfight in the Blixenesque sense, Jacob Paludan guides the story of Otto mercilessly from first to last, and it is tempting to say that Otto is up for the aesthetic necessity, knowing that otherwise there would be no story.

The route to suicide

Otto takes just over a day to go the whole way. He starts out in the Copenhagen free-port area of Frihavn, where he looks at ships, then he stops at a bar and drinks whisky. Back in the city centre he has a meal at a good restaurant, after which he tries to get some rest at Palace Hotel, in vain, leaving again after a few hours. It is now late evening, and he goes to his office; a miracle *might* have occurred. His evening continues at the Tory Club, an upmarket place of entertainment. Thus is Otto's farewell to Copenhagen. He then drives towards the Gedser ferry terminal on the south coast of Zealand, but realises that he has forgotten to bring the weights from the Bornholm clock, so he takes a room at a hotel in the small market town of Haarløv, in the Køge district on the east coast of the country. He continues his journey next morning, ending up in a seaman's hangout in Helsingør, on the north coast. After a long gaze at the ferry to Sweden, he drives inland through the interior of north Zealand, heading towards the small restaurant that will be his last stop before the marsh pool.

The ambivalence of escape

Just before driving to the port of Frihavn, Otto pays off the balance due on his life insurance policy and writes a note for his secretary intimating the route he is about to take: he has to leave immediately to visit a friend who is dying in Korsør, a ferry town on the west coast of Zealand! Pulling in the other direction are the forgotten weights from the clock, which would have taken him down to the seabed. He occasionally allows his attention to concentrate on more 'banal' matters; at one point, for example, he studies in detail an article about constructing small sailing boats, and when approaching his final destination he notices that there is no radio aerial on the café flagpole.

Otto is both hiding and preserving himself. He takes refuge at the good restaurant and at the Tory Club, but the waiters know nothing about what is going on and treat him as the reputable lawyer. Here he is still a respected man! His escape, while wanting to remain in the fold, is elegantly summed up in the seaman's hangout in Helsingør when he hears Lily's missing-person announcement on the radio: "Otto felt relieved. He and society were still on good terms, and he was an object of its gracious solicitude."[87] Otto almost feels like a highly-esteemed member of society, and he exhibits totally normal behaviour when telling the waiter in a man-to-man aside that the radio announcement was merely an anxious wife's call for help to track down a husband who had gone slightly off the rails. This is a clever line of defence, given that the waiter had immediately recognised Otto from the description given on the radio, but the situation also illustrates powerful resourcefulness in a desperate situation.

It is not only the waiter's reaction that highlights this distinctive physical appearance. When a member of Otto's office staff telephones the hospital in Korsør to hear if he has actually been to visit a critically ill friend, the response is emphatic: no gentleman of that appearance had been at the hospital. Otto cannot be mistaken for anyone other than himself; he is recognisable everywhere he goes – being grossly overweight, but also being a personification of the general delusion of society.

Otto is forever putting himself in 'normal' situations, adding to a picture of the human difficulty in accepting that it really is 'me' who has ended up in this catastrophic situation. When you have to be your own lawyer, it is difficult to wind up the estate.

Sleuths

From the minute he embarks upon his escape, Otto has two men on his heels. They pop up at critical moments and merely stare when he approaches them. They are impossible to pigeonhole: "Both of them were dressed in gray and had no particular characteristics to mark them", but they are still inescapable, being "a couple of gentlemen with time to spare". The two men represent the parties who will now call Otto to account and can no longer be shaken off. They could be said to be a doubling-up of Orth, who has hired them to shadow Otto. Otto wonders: "Were they sleuths, or was he letting his imagination get the best of him?"

The appearance of these two men marks Otto's awareness of the hopelessness of the situation closing in on him: "It was as if they had gradually, from day to day, intruded themselves into the horizon of his consciousness." Finally, just before the final steps out into the marsh pool: "Another car came by, and it seemed to Otto that it was slowing down."[88] This prompts him to pull himself together and carry out his scheme – possibly, of course, because he thinks it is the police arriving. On the other hand, he might be picturing the two men in the car, and thus feel compelled by his own hopeless situation.

The final night

In Dostoevsky's *Crime and Punishment*, villain and libertine Svidrigailov, who is an expert in deception, spends his final night before committing suicide in a decidedly substandard hotel room.

At first the room is oppressively stuffy, later it is freezing cold, the smell and sounds of mice everywhere. Otto follows Svidrigailov's example and spends his last night at a miserable hotel in Haarløv, anticipating the chill of death that awaits him: "The bed was so cold that he lay shivering, with his teeth chattering [...] The shapeless eiderdown puff loomed up in the darkness like an iceberg."[89] His room at the Palace Hotel, where he had earlier tried to find rest, had been unbearably hot. The experience of unbearable heat in the one place and intolerable iciness in the other reflects Otto's fluctuating state of mind.

Svidrigailov has nightmares throughout the night, beset by his worst sins. This is not the case for Otto; when he finally falls asleep he sleeps like a log and awakes refreshed. A little later he jauntily addresses a young woman he comes across feeding birds in the yard, but he cannot for a second fathom her carefree life: "[...] think of it – just feeding chickens and pigeons in Haarløv. It seemed strange."[90] Whereupon he enjoys rolling out his expert legalese when talking with the hotelier, dispelling the man's suspicions. Otto is greatly 'cheered up' by his self-defence, which is also another illustration of his ability to escape into erstwhile, normal roles.

The scene at the hotel in Haarløv is an intense depiction of the tortured individual's seamless seesaw from being filled with joie de vivre to being at an insurmountable distance from that exhilarated state. This is a precise illustration of Jacob Paludan's faculty for combining the actual events with powerful probing into Otto's mind, allowing the reader to experience the situation from Otto's vantage point and through his reactions: an iceberg eiderdown and bewilderment over the young woman's simple responsibilities!

Death before normalisation and punishment

In *Crime and Punishment*, Raskolnikov nearly drowns himself, and he makes many detours before making his confession to the police; Dostoevsky allows him to take on board the suffering, the sin and the blame. With the exception of a moment of weakness at the very end, to which we will return, it does not occur to Otto that he should make a clean breast of it. Come hell or high water, he is determined to avoid "the police, a cell, the trial, and a sentence."[91] He is desperate not to drag the family name through a drawn-out lawsuit, but this is also because a sense of guilt is alien to him. Otto will not undergo the slimming process of the cell, because a loss of weight would be an affront to his entire way of life.

As he drives away from the hotel in Haarløv, he worries about having an accident: "The roads were still slippery with frost, and he had to drive carefully. He began to wonder what was the point in being careful. Yes, because if there should be an accident he'd be caught in a trap; they would take the best possible care of him so that he could be handed over to the police in good, sound condition."[92] Otto can imagine robust efforts being made to 'heal' him before the trial and conviction. The implication of 'heal' is that he will be rendered a normal, dutiful citizen who has repented his exploits – whereupon he will be punished. The pairing of normalisation and punishment will be society's ultimate triumph.

This interpretation of the quote is inspired by a strong theory that Jacob Paludan had a story in mind – a story told by Ivan Karamazov in Dostoevsky's novel *The Brothers Karamazov* (1880). It is a story about a man who grows up a savage, later living as a social outcast until he is imprisoned and condemned to death for looting and murder. Priests and cultivated citizens rush to visit him in prison, where he learns to read and write and is introduced to the Holy Scriptures. He is pressed from all sides, kissed and embraced too; he is converted, full of repentance. His head is nonetheless neatly and fraternally severed from his body. Had the man been allowed to live, his crime would have been surmounted. By killing him as a criminal, his crime lives on, now doubled. The story is one of many appeals from Dostoevsky's pen in opposition to the death penalty.[93]

Jacob Paludan is generally extremely critical of public institutions; of prisons he writes in his novel *Birds Around the Light*: "[…] the long hours harden the soul. Prison cannot clear away criminal thoughts; it offers, instead, a fertile field for the development of such thoughts. The prisoner is sad when he goes in; when he comes out, he is vindictive. And then they speak of houses of Correction!"[94] Otto is also spared this fate; a term of imprisonment would only have made matters worse.

Otto and Alberti

A political and physical Danish heavyweight underwent the prison slimming regime that Otto avoids: "When Alberti arrived at Horsens Correctional Institution on December 20th 1910, his newly-opened file recorded that he was 188 cm tall, weighed 138½ kg and had a waist measurement of 155 cm. The prison was not accustomed to inmates of that size, so a special outfit had to be made for him […] By the summer of 1912 his weight was down to 71 kilo. He had practically stopped eating, was apathetic, and there were fears for his life" – as described by Henrik Larsen in *Alberti-Katastrofen* (1996; The Alberti Disaster).[95] The book also tells how Supreme Court attorney, Minister of Justice and major embezzler P. A. Alberti (Peter Adler Alberti, 1851–1932) was renowned for his colossal appetite and was fond of going to the trotting track. Walking along a beach in Hornbæk, north Zealand, shortly before giving himself up, Alberti had considered committing suicide. Instead, he visited a barber in Copenhagen and then went to his regular eating place for a first-rate meal, after which, smoking a cigar, he walked to the police station and handed himself in! By drawing this parallel with Alberti, Jacob Paludan is heavily underscoring his wish for 'Otto' to be of broader significance.[96]

Clarifications in the hinterland

Lily reports Otto's disappearance to his parents: his father's face promptly turns ashen. If he has been repressing his misgivings with regard to what is going on with Otto, Thorvald Stein certainly knows now, and he also undoubtedly knows that he will not be seeing his son again. He is equally aware that he has been handed his own death sentence. Otto's fraudulent transactions and his suicide were generated by his father's decline. The progress of his father's illness is an external picture of Otto's decline. The father therefore instantly understands the fate that has befallen the son; it is his fate too, and he dies shortly after Otto's suicide. Thorvald Stein buys a three-cornered Napoleon hat; with the hat on his head and his hand tucked into the breast of his jacket, he walks out into the street and is run over by a car. He has met with the same fate as Alberti, who died in the traffic on a Copenhagen street, knocked over by a tram in the summer of 1932.[97]

While following his escape route, Otto has a constant concern at the back of his mind about how things are developing 'back home'. He knows the exact moment at which he will finally be exposed, leading to the issue of a warrant for his arrest: he had arranged a meeting with Orth and Klein to look over the documents relating to Klein's financial affairs. When Otto fails to turn up for the meeting, Orth is in no doubt whatsoever about how the land lies. He is aware both of Otto's looming suicide and his fraudulent activities; the latter are swiftly verified by, among other measures, bringing Goos home from Sweden. Orth and Klein meet him off the ferry in Helsingør; Otto is in Helsingør when the ferry docks; and, well well, the two men in grey pop up too. At one and the same time, on the harbourfront in Helsingør, Otto sees Orth, Goos, Klein and the sleuths! This is an overblown and highly melodramatic tableau, and fortunately only a slight blemish on the story of Otto. The message is writ large: all exit routes are blocked.

Transit

And so Otto drives towards the marsh pool. But death has a forecourt, and in Otto's case this is the little restaurant he once visited before seeing the marsh waters for the first time, with Eva. This 'restaurant' bears no relation whatsoever to the life Otto has led in Copenhagen. It is a temperance café, and the coffee he is served is "a cup of brew that had been reheated several times". No more delicious dishes and drinks for Otto, and only the stub of a cigar left. The woman serving the coffee highlights Otto's threshold situation when she tells him the café will "have to close up soon". She is ascribed other ominous remarks: "He had come late, the woman observed." Her comment is an attempt to stop Otto's talkativeness; he is clinging to life with a barrage of chatter. More fundamentally, she is saying that Otto has been a long time coming: he has been expected ever since his first visit to the restaurant!

For a moment it seems as if there might yet be a glimmer of life ahead; the little restaurant "was still lighted". Otto's wretchedness and extreme weariness are written all over him, and the woman considers offering him a bed for the night, but she refrains because Otto also exudes the air of prosperous man-about-town and she thinks the place lacks all the niceties a man like him would expect. A simple conclusion: Otto's way of life has fatal consequences. He could have saved his life – had he been someone else. Standing at the very edge of the abyss, he buckles at the knees: "privately he was thinking that if he were offered a bed he would, in the name of God, forget that he was a Stein and face the music – arrest, sentence, and punishment. The other was so – so – there was no word to describe it."

Such a thin line divides life from death – or does it. Otto *is* a man-about-town and therefore no offer of accommodation is forthcoming, and he will not forsake his pride; to request a bed for the night would have been humiliating.

We are taken all the way inside, to the very core of Otto's being. As he leaves the café his voice echoes with profound loneliness: "Otto paid and said good-bye in a husky voice. The last hand had drawn back from him."[98]

We started out where it all now ends for Otto: his final steps into the marsh pool and shock that life is one step shorter than he had calculated. There is nothing left of the life arc Eva had measured out with her 'Ugh' when she and Otto had gazed into the darkness of the pool together.

Jacob Paludan's essay "I det skraa, øjenblændende Sollys" (In the Oblique, Dazzling Sunlight) is a lovely description of a ramble in the countryside; at the end of the essay, and of the ramble, Paludan writes: "Everything passes, all the walks and their Elysian highlights too; and just let it be thus, while the prospect of one more time is still to be anticipated."[99]

This espousal of life on the very brink is typical of Dostoevsky, particularly in his depiction of Raskolnikov, as Jacob Paludan would most certainly have noted. We witness this approach to life when, for example, Raskolnikov sees a penniless and deeply alcoholic man knocked down by a carriage in the street. He helps the man home, sends for a doctor and pays for the consultation with his very last money.

The doctor concludes that letting some blood would only prolong the man's life by a few minutes at the most. Raskolnikov replies without hesitation: "Then better bleed him!"[100] The episode leaves Raskolnikov filled with an intense delight in life. A similar delight overcomes him every time he knows he has won another hour or so in which he feels sure he will not be arrested – despite the fact that he has axed two women to death.

Summing up

If we take the broad-brush approach to Otto's brutal fortunes, then paradoxically a starting point can be located in his respectable, prosperous and socially elevated childhood home. He grows up with a sense of invulnerability, feels himself to be in a position where he can do whatever he likes, and everyone in the town of Havnstrup treats him with a respect that becomes an absolute necessity to his life. The sense of entitlement in this environment also places the pressure of expectation on Otto's shoulders: the family assumes he will pursue a brilliant career and a life of auspicious fortunes. When this childhood home falls apart, Otto is perfectly clear about what needs to be done: he will have to come into money in order to restore the family status.

Otto would rather die than stand on the sidelines. At the risk of being sucked under, he swirls into the maelstrom of the 1920s, about which his turbulent life also tells a story. Otto is simultaneously a strongly individualised and a universalised character.

Above all, Otto wants excitement and action, and he is never satisfied. His death is therefore logical: it is the only completion he can achieve. His engine runs on a large tank of imagination and colossal self-confidence, and his bodywork corresponds in size. His fatal stepping on the accelerator manifests an ingrained joie de vivre and pleasure in the fine things of life. He is also a fantasist, powered by notions of a life lived on a par with the international man-about-town, taken straight from a novel. Meanwhile, Otto's relationship with his theatre mistress Wanda and his picture-perfect marriage with Lily, which will trumpet his success, are vicious downward financial spirals.

Deep within Otto lies the fear of poverty and the lean, frugal life; a fear that lay deep within the over-consuming 1920s. Otto is a generous man by nature and he loves to lavish his munificence on others, wherein also lies a deep craving for admiration and acknowledgement.

Although this state of affairs holds many a reason to desire wealth, it is not in itself a complete recipe for 'the embezzler'. Additional ingredients are needed. In this respect, Otto's facility for absolutely *not* seeing himself as a conman is crucial. He is not guilty of anything and he does not owe anyone anything. On the contrary, he only takes back the money of which *he* has been robbed. He was born to that money, and he is therefore entitled to 'borrow' from his own forthcoming bottomless coffers. The future, in which he is wealthy, is his present; the present moment with its perils does not exist for Otto.

One of the factors underpinning Raskolnikov's crime is his notion that he has the Übermensch entitlement to commit it in the first place. A 1920s' version of the 'superhuman' theory, and another element in the conman's makeup, is Otto's belief that he has exceptional talents and that talents have to be utilised without restrictions imposed by petty considerations of funding. A financial genius has to prosper, does he not. This context necessitates a total lack of empathy with his victims; Otto is not hindered by empathetic hesitation.

A talent for fraud is, of course, also a prerequisite; Otto has this skillset. When it comes to identifying a victim, he has the precision of a heat-seeking missile. He can make even the flimsiest security bond seem to be extremely favourable. His powers of persuasion and his psychological radar are first-rate. Otto can be the picture of trustworthiness and humility, and he can convince his clients that the financial world is but eagerly awaiting their entrance. The clients puff up self-importantly and are putty in Otto's hands; he can make them agree to anything in order to steal a march on rivals and not lose face. Gullibility of the prey is vital to an embezzler's existence. Finally, there must of course be a framework for the deception, and Otto is handed Goos' entire well-reputed law firm within which to operate.

Otto's context is that he *should* be growing increasingly wealthy while actually becoming poorer and poorer. This spiral is primarily allowed to run its chaotic course thanks to the conman's invincible conviction that *the* massive deal will be signed and everything will be straightened out. Another cause of the downward spiral is the conman's entrenched acceptance of the terms; Otto thus shows no actual regret and makes no explicit statement that his 'project' has not succeeded. That things can turn out like they did is all part of the show, and not in itself a failure.

In order to live the life of a conman, Otto has to pay with *his* life. Trying to provide cover for what have become wafer-thin flanks is exhausting. Even though the conman has no regrets about his deeds, the possibility of arrest is just too distressful to contemplate. Anything but that. The nature of this context precludes Otto from taking anyone into his confidence; he is thus consumed by loneliness.

Hope of saving his marriage was the only factor that could have made Otto stop. His marriage with Lily is, however, inextricably linked to the existence that collapses, and for that reason alone their union has to disintegrate. Then again, it is impossible to imagine Lily living in poverty, waiting for the return of a convict.

The upshot is a brilliant story about a man being ripped in half. He ends up in a desperate situation and takes the consequences, but his suicide is also a commitment to the life he has lived.

Jacob Paludan's narrative leads to our absolute understanding that there is no other way out for Otto. Nor could there be, given that he is also a reflection of the 1920s, leading up to the financial crash. Otto personifies the entire trajectory of that roaring decade; there is nothing for him in the dull and destitute '30s – he *is* the '20s.

The atmosphere of immutability in his childhood home is a micro picture of the stagnation in the western family just before the total disintegration brought about by the First World War. Once the smoke from the battlefields had cleared, every value lay in ruins. The moorings had ruptured and the '20s roared off on their way. This implies a strong feeling of liberty – and great liberties were taken. The duality in the Otto figure, of joie de vivre and self-destruction, are also characteristic of the drive that led the western world into the morass at the end of the 1920s.

Otto's generation has no 'father figure' from whom to take bearings, and Otto himself hands down nothing to his false son. In a way, a universe without moral values renders fraud just as good as anything else. A world devoid of moral principles is in itself a fraud. At the heart of the universalised Goos firm we see big-time conman Otto at work: a picture of the scam as a central element in our culture. Otto gambles and deceives in the spirit of the times, and in an even broader perspective he signs up to deceit as existential factor.

Otto: Rival and role model

Deceit as an existential factor that had particularly favourable conditions in the 1920s can be put into perspective, and thereby further illuminate Otto and his setting, by drawing on key concepts formulated by French literary critic and anthropologist Réne Girard (1923–2015).[101]

For René Girard, 'external mediators' guarantee that cultures are not destroyed by inner conflicts. External mediators are normative role models piloting the individual's behaviour from a sphere over which this individual has no influence. A culture with generally accepted guidelines in religious or ethical values is mediated externally, thus safeguarding against subversive rivalry between citizens.

According to René Girard, this safeguard is culturally determined whereas rivalry is a matter of human nature. Breakdown of a culture's external mediators thus leads to the breakout of rivalry. At this point 'internal mediation' steps in, meaning that the individual now finds role models in other individuals within a reachable sphere, prompting an interactive relationship.

Individuals adapt behaviour according to role models for the simple reason that imitation *is* an aspect of human nature; the core incentive in this behaviour is, according to René Girard, desire.

People are motivated by desire, and the route forward is via imitation. It is not possible to desire something autonomously, but only something desired by someone else. René Girard calls this 'mimetic desire', and the three identified stages – the subject (the person desiring) only reaches the object (whatever is being desired) by imitating a mediator (the role model for the desire) – map out a triangle, hence the term 'triangular desire'.

The 'objects' are all the elements that make up a life, everything from things to lifestyles. Mimetic desire means that the mediator's status as ideal quickly starts to alternate with the role of rival, simply because desire for the same object creates a competitive relationship.

In a world without an external regulatory framework, the battle lines are drawn for conflict among subjects, strife determined by the dialectic between imitation and rivalry. The permanence of desire is predicated on the mediator's role as 'ideal' showing the way to fulfilment of the desire, and in the other role, as 'rival', impeding that fulfilment, which would of course eradicate the desire.

From René Girard's viewpoint, therefore, rivalry is natural; and he sees violence as the natural ultimate consequence of this rivalry. His analyses of primitive societies show how internal rivalry is avoided by putting blame for the whole wretched business on a single scapegoat.

Internal mediation gains a footing with secularisation, and René Girard sees a culmination in Russian nihilism and an exemplary depiction of rivalry in Dostoevsky's novels. The fading of external mediators merely accelerates up to the First World War, reaching rock bottom in the 1920s. We see 'fatherlessness' portrayed with desperate consequences in *Jørgen Stein*, and in Otto we have a (Dostoevsky-inspired) individual who experiences the full impact of these consequences.

In René Girard's conceptual framework, Otto can be said to represent the rival modern man and his deceit is a modern form of (natural) violence. Given that all culturally-conditioned regulators had disappeared in the 1920s, rivalry and deceit could operate in unadulterated form. For the imitating person, who like Otto desires affluence, there is only one real mediator (left) by means of which to achieve this goal: the conman! As father figure, only the Alberti-type remains.

The portrait of Otto as someone who will never settle for the present circumstance, but always wants to move on, is also a picture of the unremitting spiral of desire. Otto is the 'desiring subject' and his ambitions are therefore neverending.

Triangular desire can be identified in Otto's approach to his lifestyle. He finds one of his mediators in French fiction – novels from which he draws role models for life as a European man-about-town with the women of his dreams, Wanda and Lily. He also seeks guidance from status symbols and the tabloid press. The opposite arc is particularly interesting: Otto as mediator for the others. As seen by family, colleagues, clients, his overall setting, Otto is the 'role model'!

Repercussions

In *Buddenbrooks*, Johann Buddenbrook refrains from taking legal action against his deceitful ex-son-in-law Grünlich. This could be out of consideration for the family, particularly his grieving divorced daughter, but the actual reason is that to take action would mean Kafkaesquely launching a lawsuit against himself given that Grünlich personifies the deceit at the heart of the German business culture of which Buddenbrook is the flagship. At the same time, Johann Buddenbrook is definitely not interested in revealing just how thoroughly he has been conned by Grünlich. The very same logic spares the Stein family from being dragged into a scandal after Otto's death. A stream of incoming bills from upmarket shops and restaurants, where Otto had made his purchases on credit, but not a single crime reported to the police by the countless victims of his deceit, and the newspapers remain silent as the grave on the matter.

In view of the deep symbolism connected to the bottomless marsh pool, perhaps Jacob Paludan should have let Otto vanish in the waters forevermore. But his body is recovered and cremated: "Then came the day when, out at the Bispebjerg Cemetery, Otto was transformed into the calcium and magnesium that are so much more resistant than the human personality".[102] The narrator uses Otto's death to make general modernist comments on the transient nature of the human being, but expends a great deal of ink establishing that in Otto's case this was an extraordinary speedy vanishing trick: "The dead ride swiftly, and Otto rode remarkably fast. His personality seemed to dissolve when one tried to call it to mind."[103] Otto not only evaporates in the narrator's mind, but also from the thoughts of every character in the book. A danger to all, he is well and truly repressed. The intense energy spent on erasing Otto is glaringly out of proportion to the force with which he blazes into the reader's consciousness as, in the laudatory words of literary scholars Anne-Marie Mai and Stig Dalager, "a really lifelike character".[104]

Otto's falsehearted side has the final word: Jørgen, carrying his brother's urn, meets Leif on the train heading for Havnstrup. During a long wait at a stop en route, they leave the train for a drink in the station restaurant and lose track of the time; the train is about to depart, and the urn, which they had left in the compartment, nearly travels on without them. The dead ride swiftly.

In the company of the urn, Jørgen feels that he is travelling with death itself, and Leif is no less affected by the situation: "there were dark forces within Leif's personality that exerted negative pressures – a strange and stubborn destructiveness."[105] Leif's inner life is said to be pulled down by heavy weights, so in his persona we retrieve the grandfather clock weights that Otto had planned to use for his suicide. Now ash, Otto has become sheer destruction. Leif comes very close to following him, but is saved by his relationship with Lily, Otto's widow.

After the funeral Jørgen licks his wounds by deciding to read old newspapers, which he borrows in great piles from the libraries. He goes back in time, reading through events day by day, ending where the novel opened: the Sarajevo telegram. Completely absorbed in the progressively older items of news, he suddenly happens upon his brother: "He came across a paragraph about Otto – 'the able young attorney . . .' It was like getting back to a more innocent world." With his printing-ink immersion in the past, Jørgen desperately attempts to hang onto the innocence and harmony that Otto's story has emphatically revealed to be an illusion. The description of Jørgen's trip down nostalgia lane is somewhat drawn out, but there is an elegance to his leafing through the pages, "time itself swept through him like a sighing wind".[106] The sighing is transmitted to the reader, and in a flash of light we see the graceful arc of Otto's story, from the 1914 starting shot in Sarajevo to the 1928 January evening when a 36-year-old lawyer takes the epoch with him into the waters of the marsh.

From fluff to world-class

Some authors write brilliantly from beginning to end; not a jarring note, not a mistimed word, simply a nonstop joy to read. Other authors write well and solidly, but remain on an even keel; no missteps, indeed, but no pinnacles either, and not a great deal in which to take delight. And then we have the master of unevenness, Jacob Paludan.

Not only Jørgen, but most of the characters in the novel are weakened by elaborate and florid descriptions. This is never the case when Otto is in the frame. Then the language is precise, direct and candid. The other characters are not without their troubles, but nothing in Otto's league. Otto is in a constant life-and-death situation, and Jacob Paludan's forte is clearly in capturing a character in pursuit of this destiny. The more dramatic, the thinner the ice, the better is Jacob Paludan the writer. The picture of Otto is exceptionally streamlined, with few superfluous words. When dealing with most of the other characters, Jacob Paludan has a tendency to long-windedness: for example, Otto's brother-in-law, Harald Jensen, does not like him, which we are told, without further clarification, about one million times in the novel – it is incomprehensible that this was allowed to slip through. Much else could have been cut back to the benefit of the whole. In this respect, Jacob Paludan is extremely modern, given that novels in our day, Danish and non-Danish alike, are generally several hundred pages too long.

Jacob Paludan, who industriously evaluated others in reviews and essays, lacked the capacity to evaluate himself. The authors from his period who are today more celebrated were perhaps simply better at pruning.

The story about Otto is unsentimental from start to finish, even though Jacob Paludan had quite a penchant for sugariness. It is unusual to read a novel that is one moment pure fluff writing and the next moment soars to world-class status. The fluctuations are a source of irritation, but it is actually a rather interesting phenomenon. Let us look at a few examples of the fluffiness.

Nanna is one of the group of young women from whom Jørgen can take his pick. She is the sweet, unsophisticated, considerate and socially inferior girl from Aalborg. She is the daughter in the household where Jørgen takes lodgings, and he teases and flirts with her all day long. This is heady stuff, and we read, for example: "How flushed and hot her cheeks were, and how she trembled. Taking hold of her was like putting a hand down into straw and coming in contact with a litter of small, warm puppies."[107] Although highly amusing, the words verge on inexcusable overload and saccharine metaphor.

Hard to believe, perhaps, but it gets worse. Leif is in love with a lively young woman called Viola. She is not interested in anything serious, but has a girlfriend, Lise, who would very much like to get serious with Leif. One evening, when the three are together, Viola disappears and Leif is obliged to walk Lise home, but "it was in keeping with the devilish facts of existence, which always bring the wrong people together, that when the time came for them to say good-bye her expression was as genial as a dish of oatmeal with a lump of butter in the middle of it."[108] This is something of a mouthful, a heavily over-egged metaphor for a facial expression.

The desire for muscle flexing recurs in many formulations and all the way into word constructions. When two individuals meet one another unexpectedly, their "exclamations of surprise came simultaneously", and a capricious young woman has a smile that seems, on a second meeting, "doubly white and enticing".[109] Jacob Paludan cannot resist the temptation, but his love of playing with words can also pay off. There are passages in which the extravagant prose is appropriate. In the description of a consul, for example, a spirited man despite a severe debility acquired by means of a luxuriant lifestyle, whose "double chin hung down over his collar like a quilt draped over a clothesline."[110] In this instance, Jacob Paludan is maintaining the balance; the metaphor has not been hunted for high and low, but accurately encapsulates the consul's easy-going disposition in a physically challenging situation. The metaphor befittingly sums up an entire character in a both amusing and tragic way. Jacob Paludan is good at men-about-town, and the following characterisation of Customs Inspector Berg could almost be aimed at an entire type: "Berg, an overfed, heavy-set man with a complexion like a blood orange".[111] Jacob Paludan is also fond of putting a poetic turn to his sentences, and this too is most successful when applied in situations where life is being lived. Where a drink's "aroma rose fragrantly from the glasses, and it was as smooth as bottled sunshine",[112] and where "a glass of brown liqueur stood rooted to the tablecloth like a flower",[113] the reader instinctively conjures up images of paintings by Peter Severin Krøyer (1851–1909): "Ved frokosten" (1883, Artists' Luncheon at Brøndum's Hotel) and "Hip, Hip, Hurra" (1888, Hip, Hip, Hurrah!).

Parody of modern types is also one of Jacob Paludan's fortes – especially in the case of electrician Frederiksen who has recently returned home from America and is now always in a "'come on' or 'hurry up' mood", and who "even while sitting in his chair, gave the impression of only marking time before getting up and leaving." Frederiksen must submit to being sized up with a sharp pen in just a very few words: "The electrician was fresh as a daisy the whole day long".[114]

The tension Otto brings into play disappears when Jørgen enters. Jørgen is far from being a fascinating figure like Otto; on the contrary, he is stolid, very otherworldly in his thinking and speaking, and not a very pro-active person. This causes unevenness, but are there any good explanations for this, any justice for Jørgen?

Niels Barfoed, at any rate, engenders sympathy for Jørgen's situation by commenting that Otto has "the epic life" because he has "a destiny, albeit leading to a bad end",[115] whereas Jørgen has no destiny. Lack of a fascinating destiny is a modern condition, it could be added, and thus Jørgen is just as much a child of his time as is Otto.

Danish author Tage Skou-Hansen (1925–2015) has the same thought. In *Jørgen Stein* he sees the old world order break down and a modern solitariness emerge, in which the individual has been incapacitated from taking action.[116] Even though he does not name him directly, Skou-Hansen supplies a framework for understanding Jørgen's inability to act. Danish author and literary critic Paul la Cour (1902–1956) writes that the Stein brothers shed light on their day and age from two angles: "Otto represents the family's financial and Jørgen its cultural bankruptcy".[117] As in the work of Søren Kierkegaard, 'family' can here mean 'society', and Paul la Cour thus makes all Jørgen's futile talk expressive of a general lack of 'culture'. Paul la Cour can be backed up by reference to D.H. Lawrence's novel *Lady Chatterley's Lover* (1928), in which an incredible amount of empty dialogue is expressive of the void in Great Britain after the First World War.

Jørgen is immobilised, because the times are immobilised; his words are empty, because everything has become pointless. In contrast, Otto lives in a world of drama; but it all amounts to the same thing, because the drama simply leads to a bad end. Despite their many differences, the brothers share a lack of anchorage in their present day – the era bequeaths no raison d'être to either of them.

Although this is a stout defence of the Jørgen figure, he still does not take off as a fictional character in the same palpable manner as Otto, who has his destiny mapped out in the dramatic storyline that is Jacob Paludan's true element, and about which Danish literary historian Ernst Frandsen (1894–1952) employs lofty words: "On Otto's story the author has expended the sum of his skill for disposition, the crack and crash are classic plot-driven fiction without an eye to cheap effects."[118] It is the real timeless deal, according to Ernst Frandsen, and therefore hardly surprising that the reader is captivated. It is important to add that Jacob Paludan *tunes* this form, rendering it in sync with aspects of fraud that are typical of his time and typical of all time. It is a classic plot-driven novel in a modern version.

Jacob Paludan, circa 1933. Photograph: Kehlet.

PART II

Genesis of Otto in Jacob Paludan's Novels

The parrot and the mites

Jacob Paludan's first published novel, *De vestlige Veje* (1922; The Western Roads),[119] opens in the United States just after the First World War. A Danish emigrant, Harry Rasmussen, moves away from his wife and homestead, heading to the city in the hope of employment for the winter while work at home lay idle. His wife would seem to have been left all alone at the back of beyond, no friends or family are mentioned, which is a plausible reason for her disappearance: when Harry arrives home after his six months of hard work, he is greeted by a thick layer of dust inside the house, but not so much as a word from his wife.

The loneliness that overwhelms Harry points towards Otto's loneliness at his moment of suicide: "Harry stood up slowly and went to stand in the doorway. Outside, the prairie lay blueish-green in the light of the setting sun. He stared for a long time into the vast loneliness. The loneliness that closes around anyone who dives in, with not a bubble, not a ring in the water."[120]

Harry signs on as a sailor, which takes him to South America where he signs off in the fictive country of Selenia, in reality Ecuador, where he gets a job with a Danish export company. He meets all manner of business people, and they are all treated with a sharp satirical pen. The Americans only talk about: "Dollars, about share prices, about making money. When they mentioned the word dollars they got the same look in their eyes as a Catholic gets when he mentions the Virgin Mary."[121] Japanese, Chinese and German businesses stayed open day and night, the top three on the endless list of modern workaholics of whom it is written: "The hard workers will not reach a round total until their days of life do too, when deals and detestation come to a close for evermore."[122]

Otto's round-the-clock work is its own parody of the workaholic, but at the same time he commits fraud in order to procure his gold here and now and thereby sidestep the treadmill as described in *De vestlige Veje*: "In Selenia [...] you work until you pass out, to lay the financial foundations for the big house and the limousine. Your best years are squandered so you can preside over the pleasures of life when you can no longer enjoy them."[123]

Deceit is thus the rule from the outset, albeit in Paludan's first novel there is an exception: Harry is determined to have one living being in his orbit who is *not* deceitful, and so he buys a parrot. People use any means by which to accrue more, constantly, with the upshot that work is driven by dissatisfaction: "the only thing worth owning is that which is unattainable [...] the moon is what we want".[124]

It was bad enough in Selenia, but things get worse when Harry arrives in New York, where the unemployed are left to their own devices, unless they let themselves be remodelled into military fighting machines, and the homeless die in the streets. *De vestlige Veje* is a harsh and straightforward novel with no words of redemption. In *Crime and Punishment*, Raskolnikov murders a female pawnbroker, thereby to stamp out evil in society. In *De vestlige Veje*, Harry observes: "On Third Avenue, the pawnbrokers live as densely as mites in a cheese."[125]

No mercy to be had, and to an extent that Jacob Paludan almost seems to be excusing the people from whom Otto derives: "If you're not ruthless and brutal here, you'll go to the dogs."[126] Having overcome a period of intense homesickness, Harry eventually decides to stay in the United States. He has come to an understanding that being in the US or in Denmark all comes out the same in the end. *De vestlige Veje* is a novel about the entire western world. The crash of 1929 and subsequent collapses are predicted as the most natural of developments: "A little contraction in the money market is enough to send thousands of unemployed people onto the streets [...] Every seventh year disaster strikes: people behave like wild animals, go into the shops and offer to work for half of what the current staff earn. A deft operation, driving up the buying power of money. Who profited?"[127]

Suicide fish

In his next novel, *Søgelys* (1923; Searchlight), Jacob Paludan gives a clear picture of what Harry could have expected had he returned home to Denmark. War veteran Hugo Fahlen is so deeply disappointed by his welcome that he regrets not staying on the battlefield or jumping overboard before the ferry reached the harbour of his homeland, about which he had dreamt so passionately in the trenches.

Long before *All Quiet on the Western Front* (1929),[128] Hugo warns us of the horrors:

> "Have you any idea [...] what poison gas is like?" He had to speak: "It's a brown mist that settles slowly and starts to choke you. It lies on its stomach across the battlefield and has time to spare, gradually sending its fingers down through the chambers of the trenches, ten thousand fingers with sharp nails! People lurch towards it, and then it thrusts a nail down into their lungs [...] There are mustard-gas shells too. Dropped into a cluster of men as they stand talking about dinner and making feeble puns. Then: whuzz! And the men flail around, bellowing, their whole bodies on fire, blind and deaf, screaming like stuck pigs [...]."[129]

Hugo is suffering severely from shell shock and post-traumatic stress disorder, the least sound from the street frays his nerves. His mind can be utterly empty for days on end, or he has "explosions in his brain"[130] and nightmares.

After the war, he struggles through a tough period of unemployment in New York before finally being hired as a driver at a gunpowder factory, consoling himself with the thought that explosives are also used for peaceful purposes – and another war is surely not an option. Hugo returns to Denmark with only enough money to last a month; in line with Otto, his mantra insists it will all turn out fine as long as the next step looks reassuring: just like the pipe of tobacco you managed to enjoy in safety behind the frontline.

When the money has all gone, a touch of forgery secures Hugo a loan, giving him a "little breather […], some sunrises, some streets with people in them." His dishonesty is followed by new suicidal thoughts, kept in check by: "the flesh, which without being asked and on its own account contested annihilation."[131] In Hugo's case, this objection does not materialise corporeally in mountains of flesh.

Hugo takes things no further than this one case of fraud; he had just the one chance to wave his magic wand. He overhears a telephone conversation that makes him realise he has been found out. This time he takes a real step towards suicide. He goes to the shore near the H. C. Ørstedsværk power station in Copenhagen, and Jacob Paludan decides to let us see the suicide as Hugo imagines it will be, as he stands on the steps leading down into the ice-covered water:

> All he had to do was walk down the steps and onwards, out onto the white floor, out towards the buoys sticking up through the ice like oblique brooms, onwards, until it creaked, onwards until it cracked. An ice floe rears up, he slips and vanishes. The lid closes, airtight and exact. Nighttime and desolate, nothing has happened. And then – long silence, endless bubbling darkness […].[132]

It goes no further than the pictured phase, and we are spared an actual trip down into the bubbling darkness, although Jacob Paludan takes his revenge when it is Otto's turn – had he perhaps been irked by wasting his chance in *Søgelys*?

Standing 'safely' on the steps, Hugo cannot sink into the water one stride earlier than calculated, and he has time to see what is in store if he keeps going: "He [...] looked at the bottom step, at something strange. Just a dead fish that had been washed ashore [...]."A potential suicide seeing himself as a dead fish is rather heavy-duty, but the balance is maintained, particularly with the added information that the curve of the fish looks like a question mark.

With a sentimentality that is passé in the picture of Otto, Hugo answers the question via thoughts of an Ecuadorian doctor who had both his feet amputated in a traffic accident; Hugo is filled with joy that he has the use of his limbs. His spirits return, "he looked fearlessly out into the darkness" and is rewarded by "lights glinting at him from a little café",[133] a situation in which Otto finds no help just before his suicide when he sees the "little restaurant that was still lighted".[134]

Otto does not accept punishment, but Hugo does. He takes "the shortest route to the police station",[135] a decision prompted by bumping into an acquaintance, Edith, on the street; she has previously, and on several occasions, reminded Hugo of his value as a person. Edith serves the same function as Raskolnikov's girlfriend Sonya, who stops the murderer on the street in St Petersburg and persuades him to go to the police, after which she accompanies him to Siberia, where she is his light in the darkness.

Edith and Hugo live in the same boarding house; on one of the occasions when she is telling him about all his many possibilities in life, he is so inspired by her homily that a waltz springs into his mind. He immediately writes it down, and it is later accepted by a music publisher. While he is in prison Hugo learns that his waltz tune has become a hit. Its title is "I

Lys vi færdes" (We Move in Light), and the light ahead for Hugo might very well be Edith, to whom he has made over the copyright to his composition.

Søgelys involves a suicide that could have played a role for one of Jacob Paludan's colleagues, Danish poet and novelist Tom Kristensen (1893–1974). The suicide occurs within the orbit of a gossip columnist called Erup. He writes "surface froth"[136] in the newspaper *Klokken et* (One o'clock) and now feels "as empty as a blown-out egg".[137] Browsing in a bookshop one day, he finds a poetry collection, *Syner* (Apparitions), written by Eigil Holm, a friend from his young days. The work is "so unknown to everyone, it was as if it had never existed". It has, in a sense, only existed in Erup's imagination, because Eigil Holm personifies Erup's unrealised dreams of becoming a poet. Eigil Holm committed suicide by hanging himself when he and Erup were both still young; an act that proved to be Erup's *literary* suicide. Hope of resuscitation surfaces when Erup finds the copy of *Syner*, thinks "we must buy your freedom, old friend"[138] and contemplates digging out the poems he wrote when he was young. This hope is short-lived; he ends up staying on the career trajectory that has led him away from poetry.

Syner knocks on Erup's door, and in all probability Tom Kristensen had an eye to *Søgelys* when his character Steffen Steffensen knocks on the door of established literary editor Ole Jastrau in his major novel *Hærværk* (1930; *Havoc*, 1968). Although Steffensen does not commit suicide, he is similarly the personification of Ole Jastrau's neglected dreams of becoming a poet. Tom Kristensen might well have found inspiration for *Hærværk* in the well-designed and amusing picture of life on a daily newspaper we are shown in *Søgelys*.

The end of winter life

In Jacob Paludan's third novel, *En Vinter lang* (1924; Winter Long), qualified pharmacologist Keller fails to fulfil his ambition of a career in science; this plunges him into a peripatetic life working in the one pharmacy after the other. He pulls up his roots and drifts around like a friendless nomad.

Keller believes everything to have changed when he meets the great love of his life in Ethel; she, however, wants to be an actor, a prospect he cannot accept, and so their relationship breaks down. The split is also the result of Keller's preference for dodging involvements that require commitment. Having broken up with Ethel, he settles in the small market town of Vejstrand, a name that resonates with his situation: he is stranded on his route through life.[139] Keller has withdrawn deep into himself, a state underscored by the total absence of letters arriving in his postbox. After ten years in Vejstrand, Keller's winter life thaws out and the depiction of this process is the actual storyline, beginning in January when "all sun is forgotten"[140] and ending in May. The year is 1919, and this novel too addresses post-war rootlessness.

The now middle-aged Keller falls in love with a ray of springtime sun, Sofie, a young assistant at the pharmacy where he works. Sofie returns his love, and she sees it as her mission to break Keller's chains and heal his wounds.

Sofie represents all that is healthy, she flows with "the charitable powers of life",[141] which now gush forth in Keller, and he no longer feels like a guest in Vejstrand: "He went from the barren phase to the fertile [...] everything seemed to bid him welcome [...] it was good to reach the point of being able to call something his when he had been a tourist for as long as he could remember".[142] Tangible signs of change include Keller's new clothes and his letter-writing.

The story is left open in that Sofie also turns out to be the arrival of springtime for another and younger man; on the other hand, at the very end of the novel, Keller receives a letter from her, accompanied by hyacinths, symbolic of concord and budding love. Sofie would seem to represent the coming of spring for everyone.

It is highly likely that another major Danish author, Martin A. Hansen (1909–1955), drew on *En Vinter lang* for his novel

Løgneren (1950; *The Liar*, 1995). *The Liar* takes place on the island of Sandø, the symbolic meaning of which is similar to that of 'Vejstrand'. On Sandø, 'sand island', the forty-year-old dreamer Johannes Vig is well 'sanded up'. Despite spending seven years on the island, he has yet to be on firm ground. He is like a faraway island, alone in the world and forgotten by all; nor does *he* receive letters.

Johannes Vig's reluctance to become involved is also due to his difficulty in accepting that humankind has to keep on leaving new footprints even though everything is sand: an existential feeling, but with a historical dimension. Johannes Vig struggles with "an after-the-war mentality, finding everything senseless"[143] – the difference here being that it is after the Second World War, whereas *En Vinter lang* is set after the First World War.

Likewise, *The Liar* both depicts Johannes Vig's 'winter state' and his 'spring breakthrough'. He froze over and took up residence on Sandø as a consequence of a wounded emotional state and unfulfilled ambitions. His grand passion was accompanied by the desire to be a learned man: "Yet for a time, a whole year, I was in the seventh heaven of delight, because it was Birte and I, and I was studying literature too."[144] When Birte dropped him, he dropped out of university, and studied to be a school teacher instead, which is now his job on Sandø.

For seven years Johannes Vig has felt like a guest – a 'migratory bird' – on Sandø. He only declares his love to Anne Marie when he knows it is too late, even though she has been willing for many years. Johannes Vig does not want to be tied down, because that equals 'unrest'.

Johannes Vig gradually recognises that his 'migratory-bird existence' is untenable, and he is eventually ready to commit himself. He leaves his footprints by means of a large written work on the topography of Sandø, and he lets a pregnant unmarried barmaid move in, with all the ensuing 'unrest'. This is clearly symbolic of spring, life, breaking forth in

Johannes Vig and asserting its rights. Letters immediately start arriving, and on Sandø he no longer feels like a stranger: "It was the first time that I had stood here on Western Hill and realized that my fate was bound for always to this hill in the sea [...] I am no longer a visitor here, but a man in his proper place."[145]

Face to face

The protagonist in Jacob Paludan's fourth novel, *Fugle omkring Fyret* (1925; *Birds Around the Light*, 1928), is Johan Brandt, son of the lighthouse keeper in Sandhavn on the west coast of Jutland. We follow his formative years leading to adulthood, from pre-First World War and into the 1920s, the same period during which Jørgen Stein has to become a man. Johan Brandt's development runs hand-in-hand with the construction of a harbour in Sandhavn and the compulsory purchase of the harbour hinterland, which changes the life of the town. Like Jørgen Stein, Johan Brandt spends a lot of time pondering the ways and waywardness of life and love – somewhat long-windedly. In the lawyer Herluf Nagel we have a subordinate character whose route to suicide is mapped in an incisive and fascinating way.

The story of Herluf Nagel has its own particularity, but also elements clearly applicable to Otto.[146] Nagel is also a speculator, for example, willing to enrich himself at the expense of others without the least sympathy for his victims; they must accept his simple philosophy: "All life is a risk."[147] Apart from the very end of the story, to which I shall return, Nagel is 'only' tarnished in a moral sense – he uses shady tricks, but he cannot be called an embezzler in the legal sense.

Nagel is the first to realise that the harbour construction project will be followed through and so he buys up land, which he then sells on with a large profit. The buyers, on the other hand, end up with egg on their faces when the government expropriates the land but only pays them half the price they paid Nagel. Nagel also takes the opportunity to purchase land that he will sell for even greater profit once the harbour is operational and the town is ripe for development.

The incentive underlying Nagel's wheeler-dealering is his pursuit of the 'sweet life'. He is a talented and sly fox, but a lazy and uncommonly handsome man who had no trouble getting himself a wife with a large dowry: "When they went to the altar Mammon had stood priest."[148] Therefore, he merely needs to keep his law firm afloat and safeguard his future through his activities as a speculator.

In contrast to Otto's relationship with Lily, Nagel does not love his wife, Mathilde, although she idolises him, but the two marriages are similar in their total lack of any stimulating contact.

Nagel, too, is a man-about-town to his fingertips: "When the café coat-room attendant handed him hat and fur coat, and he stood with half-closed eyes, carefully lighting a cigar, conversation stopped at nearby tables. His clothes, his habits, the topic was inexhaustible."[149] Jacob Paludan is again in his element when handling the man-about-town – who becomes a suicide – here with extremely precise descriptions of Nagel's pleasure in food, drink and smoking, subtle details, nothing superfluous. While the *whole* of Otto's body gradually reflects the costs, Nagel's destruction can as yet only be read in his face: "His face revealed that he had tasted all of life's joys that can be purchased by good health."[150]

Nagel's decline speeds up when Mathilde dies, and the last of her dowry money is used to pay for her funeral. He then has to buy on credit, but he is convinced that his law business will flourish; like Otto, he also anticipates the event that will facilitate his recovery at one fell stroke. In Nagel's case this will be the opening of the new harbour: "An unfortunate combination of unfavorable circumstances was to blame for it all. But the ceremonies of this day, and the ensuing sensation of Sandhavn's financial condition, would change all for the good. Who could tell; mayhap the first buyers for his land were already on their way."[151]

This is where Nagel, confident as he is in the future, oversteps the limits of the law. Otto's criminal career starts with a 'working loan' of money he ought to have paid into the account of a charitable foundation, and Nagel similarly resorts to financing the wait for new capital with money he, as lawyer, receives from a house buyer and then 'borrows' from the house vendor.

Otto is swallowed up by the 1920s' maelstrom, and Nagel's fate is also interwoven with the march of history. When a mole bursts during the opening ceremony, the waters gush in and the harbour becomes a thing of the past. Nagel faces financial ruin, and he seeks rescue from Bodil, the lead female character who, like Edith in *Søgelys* and Sofie in *En Vinter lang*, represents the stimulating life forces. Bodil is young and unspoiled, not to mention "the wild spicy herb of renewing youth . . . "[152] She is highly receptive to Nagel's 'proposal', right up until: "Slowly she opened her eyes and saw his face, a weakly grey, blistered mass."[153] She promptly shows him the door, which is clearly symbolic of Nagel's life drawing to a close.

The ensuing description of his suicide is theatrical, but that does not detract from the fascination, as always, when Jacob Paludan passes over the chatter and lets the dramatic events do the talking. Nagel hangs himself in a hotel room, displaying the same pride and inquisitiveness that Otto maintains to the very end. He thinks it important to die "completely dressed",[154] the white tie and tails he wore at the dinner held to celebrate the opening of the new harbour, and he angles the chair to the large wardrobe mirror so that he can watch himself fall. With this morbid self-observation Nagel stifles the growl of terror he heard coming from his throat during these preparations, the sound of a wild animal.

Enterprising women

Markerne modnes (1927; The Fields are Ripening), the last novel Jacob Paludan wrote before *Jørgen Stein*, is set during and a few years after the First World War. *Markerne modnes* is the story of a friendship between a miller's son called Ivar and a landowner's son called Ralf. Ralf represents everything Ivar desires of life. Ivar is in love with Ralf's sister Bettina, and marriage with her would give right of entry to that picture of his ideal life. Bettina is more than interested in Ivar, making no secret of the fact and advising him of a fundamental rule: "If you never learn to take for yourself, Ivar, then others will take from you."[155]

Ivar wavers between becoming a doctor or a musician; Bettina is ready to be the violinist's muse. He does not, however, take her for himself, and so she immediately takes a singer instead, because she is where the music plays. Ivar chooses Ellinor, Ralf's and Bettina's cousin; in so doing, the music is taken from him: Ellinor states categorically that if he wants to marry her then he must burn all his sheet music – which he does. Ivar chooses 'the cousin' in preference to 'the sister', thereby distancing himself from what he really desires of life.

Ivar has an operation on his middle finger; two joints are removed, which is a somewhat contrived strategy to take him away from his violin. His afflicted finger and the surgery occur while, of course, he is capitulating to Ellinor and withdrawing from Bettina. So it is entirely his own fault.

Ellinor wants to be a doctor's wife, which is what she becomes. Even so, she is dissatisfied with Ivar's efforts, complaining that he earns less than he could, and she has a point because his unrealistic dreams of becoming a musician slow him down. He tries to speed up by taking 'stimulants' from the medicine cupboard, and before long he is addicted, a morphinist. Ellinor craves comfort, expensive cars, travel, holidays at fashionable resorts, and so on and so forth; she is "the daughter of a new and liberated time", willing "life to be enjoyed before it withers away"[156] – in this demand for the material things in life, she resembles Lily, Otto's wife.

Ellinor is the price an artist pays if he lets himself be

swallowed up by worldly matters. Her worldliness is steeped in sexuality, which renders Ivar defenceless from the very first time she makes a move on him: "she threw her arm around his shoulders. Ivar sat quite still; no bird under a hand could have sat quite as still as the grave."[157] This kind of subjugation to sexuality is not helpful to the aspiring artist; the necessary parameters for creative sublimation would have been possible with Bettina, who is not quite so feisty.

Ivar fails to pluck up the nerve to take Bettina, with the consequence that Ellinor takes Bettina from him. This is given an amusing twist when Ellinor makes advances to Bettina in several overtly lesbian scenes involving some passionate kissing. Leading Bettina up a "creaking interior stairway" to her room, for example, Ellinor "put her arm around Bettina's waist and looked forward to really kissing her on the way up". The project is thoroughly successful given that a little later: "The young women came down, flushed and laughing".[158]

Ellinor consistently takes what she wants. Having tired of Ivar she puts all her energy into Bertel, who is also a doctor, a man able to offer everything she could wish for of life as a doctor's wife. She reels him in during a splendid scene when he is summoned to attend Ivar, who is ill in bed. In the bedroom, Ellinor treats Ivar in an extremely nursing staff-sister way, which Bertel finds both irritating and highly titillating – but he is also attracted by the caring side she puts on enticing display. She proceeds to seduce him without more ado: "Then she followed after him, and in the dark corridor just outside the bedroom she grasped hold of him, her mouth sliding across his, and a stiff hat was heard rolling across the floor."[159] Bertel later takes her away from Ivar; she gets into his comfortable car, the door slams behind her and she instantly forgets all about Klara and Niels, her two children.

The erotic scenes in *Markerne modnes* are highly relevant to an understanding of the characters and their actions, as when Ralf too is taken without more ado; in his case, the driving force is a young teacher, Miss Else Bentzen:

It had come so suddenly, albeit when he pictured her light-blue, thirsty eyes he had long been caused to sigh and leaf through poetry books. Her closeness had made him uneasy; when he knew she was behind him, it was like a wave of summer heat. He could instantly feel her fiery kisses on the back of his neck; she drew him in, closer, closer; he had not known it was possible to be so close, but she had her laughing and sighing knowledge. That had been a month ago. Last night, he had been with her again, from midnight to early morning; she had called him – all manner of words, like a lava flow, pouring into his ear, her narrow bed a hearth full of glowing coals.[160]

Even though Otto's Lily is very much her own woman, her seductive and sexual features have been 'rehearsed' in Else Bentzen and Ellinor, with Lily and Ellinor also sharing a deceitful side. The delicacy and elegance, and carnality, with which Else and Ellinor are imbued run through Lily too. And yet Lily is even more sophisticated, with a gravity and depth that Jacob Paludan does not ascribe Else and Ellinor.

Ivar does not aim for total implementation of his Ralf-side, and so it comes as no surprise that the gloss wears off Ralf in the course of the novel – when he contracts syphilis, for example. Ralf's problems are revealed most profoundly in Klara, when it turns out that he is her father – and thus Ellinor has also been unfaithful to Ivar. Klara is severely disabled, both physically and mentally. Bettina's words to Ivar ring out again: "If you never learn to take for yourself, Ivar, then others will take from you." In this instance, fatherhood is taken from him – and yet not. In the form of his distorted Ralf-side, Ivar is in effect the child's father; and so it makes sense that he seriously considers liberating poor Klara with a shot from the medicine cupboard.

Ivar targets Klara because she represents the epitome of his sins of omission; we read, in fine doppelgänger style: "Today Ivar knew that love had only given him what Ralf had rejected."[161] Klara thus knows that she is in danger every time 'father' calls her in for a medical consultation, and one day she runs away just as he is thinking of calling for her. He chases after his 'daughter', the morphine capsules in his pocket; she falls into the marshy waters and he makes no attempt to rescue her:

> She ran straight towards the Rørmose marshland, which concealed its black waters behind a ridge of earth. She might fall in; he had to stop this chase. Standing still, he looked around; no, no one was watching them. He looked ahead again. She was nowhere to be seen. She must have slipped into the water. His heart started thudding loudly, dreadful beats with lengthy intervals. He gazed tensely at the straight dark bank of earth in front of him. Why did she not call out? The slightest sound would transform him from a pillar of salt into a human being leaping to assistance [...]
>
> Then Ivar saw, sharply outlined against the sky, a thin arm jut upwards, gesticulate and flap forwards. Nothing more, and not a sound. He thought the arm was threatening him, his mouth fell open. His knees gave way, he fell. In so doing, he caught sight of what he had in his hand: the powder. He feverishly broke the capsule open and inhaled the contents [...] He looked calmly towards the marshy pool, where now there was nothing to be seen, where the water must have closed again and completed its merciful deed [...] he stood up, free and happy.[162]

In thinking that the arm looks threatening, Ivar reveals his bad conscience over letting Klara, and thus a burden, sink to the bottom of the marshland pool. He numbs any pangs of remorse with morphine, and they are replaced by a profound sense of freedom that conceals the repression of guilt just like the water conceals Klara. Ivar fails to use 'Klara' as a cognitive facilitator to the unravelling of his problems and a fresh start; the extent of his resignation is plainly reflected in his choice of widow Aase Børgesen, his household help, as his new partner in life:

> A fleshiness was emerging here and there, of his cheeks too. And his collars became tighter and tighter. Oh but she was a good cook, Mrs. Børgesen. Her mock turtle soup and her apple charlotte could simply not be bettered anywhere [...] She might be a little stout and nondescript, but she had kind eyes [...] yes, well, all right, so she would do.[163]

Klara does not die in the marshy waters – although, in respect of the narrative, that would probably have been for the best. Jacob Paludan squeezes until the pips squeak by revealing that the arm was actually draped around the stem of a tree, saving Klara's life; shortly afterwards, therefore, she is able to enter Ivar's consulting room and commit suicide by drinking from "a yellow bottle".[164] Jacob Paludan had undoubtedly wanted to entertain by means of this *overkill*: the repressed element, Klara, turns up one last time merely to note that Ivar's choice has rendered her natural life unfeasible.

Wet marshland plays a regular role in Jacob Paludan's writing. Before Otto enters the marshy setting, Klara's scene is the most detailed and significant, although a story in *De vestlige Veje* comes close and Jacob Paludan must have had it in mind when he imagined Klara's arm jutting up from the marshland pool.

In South America, Harry spends a Christmas Eve with another Dane, a man called Petri, who tells him about goings-on in the countryside back home in Denmark, and particularly a trip out into the wild marshland, including a sinister account of what it would be like to disappear in the waters:

> The wild marshland is a plateau of moist banks of earth surrounding pools of gurgling water. Do not set your foot there [...] Human bodies would be ruthlessly sucked under. Imagine standing out there! You scream, but no one hears

[...] Now the mud reaches your chest, cold and slimy; you push against it, but it is impossible to tread water in dough. You have just two minutes left, for religious deliberations... [...] Right, now your nostrils and mouth are full of mud: silence. Long after your head has gone, an arm juts into the air [...] and the fingers vanish, with a contented gurgle the water erases all trace of you.[165]

Had Klara screamed, Ivar would have heard her – he was, after all, listening – but on no account would he have intervened. Unlike Klara's encounter with the marshes, Petri's story is not woven into the storyline as such, but he is nonetheless given the role of highlighting a central theme of the novel in which he is a subordinate character. His dreadful description of this route to destruction, step by step, with every prospect of encountering awful horrors along the way and no hope of help, is not only a picture of the threat of sinking without trace in South and North America, but also of going the same way should you choose to return home to the land of marshy waters.

With Jacob Paludan's partiality for marshland and his pinpoint accuracy in its use, the venue would have been an obvious choice as the element of downfall for Otto. It is said of a writer in *Markerne modnes* that "his literary forte was death scenes"[166] – this could almost be considered a self-characterisation.

Marshland is described in highly positive terms elsewhere in Paludan's writings; in his essay "On Taking Over a Cabin in Jutland",[167] for example, it is a peaceful territory "beyond the domains of busy people".[168] Here marshland is a refuge from the conventional world with its appetites and incessant activity by which Otto was so beleaguered. Jacob Paludan's thoughts around Otto's death scene undoubtedly included a notion of marshland as an element of deliverance.

Rounding off

All six of Jacob Paludan's novels deal with the times in which they were written and originally published, and all six are therefore set in the same historical period: they open before, during and just after the First World War and follow journeys up through the 1920s. This journey is, in a way, rounded off by *Jørgen Stein*, which opens before the First World War and ends in the spring of 1933.

Furthermore, dotted around the five novels leading up to *Jørgen Stein* we see many 'practice runs' of themes in which Otto is embedded. The story of Otto gives these themes a broad and overall articulation.

In general terms, these five novels are concerned with the modern business world and financial speculation in the 1920s; but they also address the common experience of 'emptiness' in a decade during which the theme of 'deceit' was applicable both to the actual historical circumstances and to the existential circumstances.

Deception also plays a role in depictions of love in the novels. Jacob Paludan has a tendency to put his female characters into one of two categories: the good, reliable but somewhat passive woman, or the deceitful, sexual and seductive woman. The latter category relates to the modern liberated woman who wishes to participate in the life of fashionable society with its amusements and material comforts. This 'sweet life' had come within reach in the 1920s, and it could be achieved via the men-about-town who flow so expertly from Jacob Paludan's pen.

The six novels all show Jacob Paludan's forte to be in the depiction of dramatic lives, the players in which are contrasted with those weak, passive and contemplative types who are somewhat lacking in the excitement stakes. The void experienced in the post-war period is also reflected in the loneliness and feeling of invalidation suffered by many of the characters. As a route out of the personal problems that always go hand-in-hand with the historical circumstances, suicide is a frequent presence in Jacob Paludan's novels; even when stopping at imagined scenarios, the suicide is always described in great detail.

Jørgen Stein was the last novel Jacob Paludan ever wrote; on the other hand, he went on to write many essay collections, and he is still considered one of Denmark's finest essayists.

PART III

Otto's Biographical Genesis

Fatherly favouritism
Stig Henning Jacob Puggaard Paludan (1896–1975) was born in Copenhagen. His mother, Gerda Puggaard (1859–1926), was the daughter of a landowner, and his father, Julius Paludan (1843–1926), was the son of a court clerk.[169] Jacob Paludan had an older brother, Hans Aage Paludan (1894–1942).

Julius Paludan had taken a degree in theology, but, as Danish literary historian Henrik Oldenburg puts it, he had "exempted himself from joining the family's lengthy list of church ministers so as to plunge into the world of literature."[170] This resulted in a famous and infamous professorship in literature: Julius Paludan was awarded the chair that everyone – apart from the university authorities – thought should have gone to the legendary Danish literary critic and author Georg Brandes (1842–1927). According to Danish literary historian Lars Peter Rømhild (1934–2020), this rendered Jacob Paludan's father "both a person of rank and an unperson in academic circles",[171] and Henrik Oldenburg is of the opinion that the entire family was severely affected because the label "conqueror of Brandes" made the father "a beaten man".[172]

Jacob Paludan himself uses the story of his father and Brandes for a literary essay in which he writes about the distinction between types of reading matter in his childhood home: the socially acceptable and the decidedly undesirable literature. He lists a number of the authors, today more or less forgotten, favoured by his father: "All very fine individuals, but, as artists, of merely passing interest to a mind ignited by literature at a young age."[173] On the other hand, when he crept into his father's vicarage-like study, cut his way through the tobacco smoke to reach the bookcase, and picked out Brandes' *Hovedstrømninger i det Nittende Aarhundredes Litteratur* (1872–1890; *Main Currents in Nineteenth-Century Literature*, Vols. 1–6, 1901–1905), the pages proved a revelation:

> It was like moving on clouds. Good heavens, this here was vivid life, everything I thought I could feel within myself – the arch-enemy was revealing *my* world, it was *these* minds to which I was drawn.[174]

Biographical treatments of Jacob Paludan generally stress the 'arch-conservative' nature of his childhood home, but Jacob Paludan himself was well-aware that it was also an arena for the classic father/son showdown, in which he mischievously pictured the arch-enemy Brandes as his ideal father – which surely did not go unnoticed by his real father.

Danish literary historian Niels Stengaard describes Julius Paludan as being "absolutely a qualified candidate for professor in aesthetics", who was actually on speaking terms with Brandes if they ran into one another at the library.[175] The story of Julius Paludan and Georg Brandes is thus also a story of challenges per se in adapting to new times and new trends.

Jacob Paludan must have felt very lonely in his childhood home. In one of his letters, he wrote that:

> there has never actually been a particularly good relationship between the old folks and me. I think there is something unique in a son being so utterly from top to bottom dissimilar to his parents, so the two sides literally cannot get through to one another and they view one another's way of being with deep-rooted suspicion.[176]

Of his father, Jacob Paludan felt able to make the sweeping statement that he represented an "obsolete world, national-ecclesiastical conservative with preterite gloss"[177] – and that his mother toed the line, so no redressing of the balance by her. This harsh judgement should be seen in the light of the father's extreme favouritism of his eldest son. The brothers had a good relationship while they were children and adolescents, they even wrote little plays together,[178] but this all ended the moment Hans Aage was old enough to be his father's confidant. In Jacob Paludan's own forlorn words, his brother ascended to the role of "idol" in the home.[179]

Jacob 'only' completed lower secondary education and 'only' trained as a pharmacist, whereas Hans Aage completed his upper secondary education, graduated from university and worked as a librarian at the Royal Danish Library (Det Kongelige Bibliotek). Henrik Oldenburg notes that Jacob Paludan "resembled a famous-family black sheep"[180] and Lars Peter Rømhild sums up: "For some years, it must have seemed to the young Stig/Jacob Paludan that his big brother was everything the home desired and got everything the conventional academic life had to give".[181]

Jacob Paludan must have found it particularly painful that even his writing failed to gain recognition from his father, the professor of literature, not even when *Birds Around the Light* was published to great acclaim in 1925; on the contrary, Jacob Paludan writes that his father had felt "Mosaic Law had been violated".[182] There are no testimonials as to how his mother and brother reacted to his writing career.[183]

Hans Aage Paludan followed the conventional route of marrying and starting a family, but Jacob Paludan remained unmarried until he was forty-seven years old. He married in 1943, one year after his brother's death, which leads Lars Peter Rømhild to pose what he calls a psychological question: "Jacob Paludan did not get married until his older brother was dead: an obstacle of some sort had passed away?"[184] More generally, Lars Peter Rømhild stresses that "for better or for worse, the fraternal relationship played a huge role for Jacob Paludan – making lengthy inroads into his writing",[185] of which this book gives a concrete example in the figure of Otto.

As far as it is possible to deduce, in terms of personality Hans Aage Paludan was far from being a model for Otto. It is nonetheless highly conceivable that Hans Aage's status in the Paludan family – the idolised and perfect son – was at the back of Jacob Paludan's mind when he created Otto: in the eyes of the Stein family, including those of younger brother Jørgen, Otto is infallible and guaranteed success. The high expectations placed on Hans Aage's shoulders might also have been passed on to Otto, for whom the consequences are described with a sympathy that could be traced back to an understanding of the problems faced by Jacob's brother in this situation.

We might go even further down the route of psychological speculation into which Lars Peter Rømhild has led us, because Jacob Paludan must also have been jealous of his brother, and it would be interesting to know if this jealousy was so intense that Otto's fall from grace entails an unconscious wish-fulfilment on Jacob Paludan's part to bring down *his* brother.

On the sidelines

In 1918 Jacob Paludan graduated in pharmacology.[186] He gave several reasons for choosing this subject, ranging from not knowing what else he should study to the choice being a reaction against his family home: "My lack of adaptation to the values handed down rendered it desirable that I remove myself elsewhere, so that my troublesome opinions did not encroach upon the everyday mood of the household."[187] This statement also indicates that the family was not upset to see Jacob Paludan pushed to the sidelines.

His studies and then his job as a pharmacist, which he pursued until 1924, took Jacob Paludan to a variety of places, even a pharmacy in Ecuador. His opinions of these workplaces vary widely. There are certainly positive elements, but in our context – with an Otto who would rather put his efforts into committing fraud than working for a regular salary – it is interesting to read Jacob Paludan's comments while he was working at Fasan Apotek, a pharmacy in the Frederiksberg district of Copenhagen:

> Take the advice of an experienced man: become a currency counterfeiter, rapist, commit perjury, smash street lamps, drink radium, rob the poor of their meagre savings […] run your wife into the ground and your children to the madhouse – but never become a pharmacist.[188]

Might not Jacob Paludan have identified a little with Otto?

Freedom of thought en plein air

Jacob Paludan's mother and father died within a few months of one another in the autumn of 1926. Despite his strained relationship with his parents, Jacob Paludan lived in his childhood home in the suburb of Frederiksberg right up until the spring of 1927 when the lease agreement expired.[189] He made frequent use, however, of boarding houses in the city and in the countryside as 'respite' from living in the family home, and he continued this pattern until 1929 when he purchased the Hestehaven estate near Hillerød and established a poultry farm.

From 1924 to 1929 two inheritances – one from an uncle and then one from his parents – made Jacob Paludan a very wealthy man. In his own words, he "could live as I pleased and work in ideal conditions".[190] Unfortunately, in the summer of 1929 disaster struck: his lawyer was revealed to be an embezzler who had lost the greater part of the capital Jacob Paludan had entrusted to his management.

In a state of deep shock, Jacob Paludan noted that "for me, this will mean a radical change of lifestyle".[191] He was resolute in his decision that under no circumstances would he return to employment as a pharmacist; nor would he attempt to live exclusively as a writer, since a writer lacking money has to prostitute himself; and under no circumstances would he live in the city with all its many temptations. So life in the countryside it would have to be, and he drew inspiration from his friend Eric Eberlin (1899–1943), who had set up a poultry farm in Sweden.

Jacob Paludan had not lost his entire fortune; he had enough money left to buy the Hestehaven property and set up a modern poultry farm, in which he saw the potential to get his finances back on track. He plunged energetically into the project, delighted by the freedom and well-being that came from working and living in the countryside. The four walls of a boarding-house room had been replaced by a spacious domain, and he found working with poultry "the most wholesome, most mind-invigorating of jobs".[192] He was particularly appreciative of his housekeeper: "Yes, I have a housekeeper [...] she is thankfully utterly beyond the age at which they get ideas, and you too, on the other hand she cooks splendid food and keeps everything spotlessly clean; all in all, a lucky find."[193]

Jacob Paludan noted that the work involved in looking after the poultry was actually not too time-consuming, so he would be able to write whenever he wanted to, should he so desire.

His enthusiasm gradually merged with a sense of loneliness and the need for "a change of horizon".[194] He had plans for a larger poultry farm with extra staff and in a less isolated location, but the ongoing world financial crisis overtook his enterprise, wiping out any hope of running a viable business. The final straw came when his housekeeper resigned and no one applied for the job; in the autumn of 1931 he abandoned the poultry farm and moved to Birkerød, a town north of Copenhagen.

Jacob Paludan lived in Birkerød for the rest of his life, working as a fulltime writer; from 1943 he lived there with his wife Vibeke Paludan (1910–1990, née Lykke Vibeke

Holck), with whom he had a son, Jens Jacob Paludan, born in 1948.

A man of many talents

In 1920 Jacob Paludan and his friend Eric Eberlin had travelled to the United States. Jacob Paludan had carried on to Ecuador and worked, as already mentioned, at a pharmacy, where he stayed for six months, before meeting up with Eberlin again in the US. For the next six months Jacob Paludan undertook various odd jobs before returning to Denmark. In 1926 he visited Eberlin in the US, where the latter lived on and off until 1928.

While working as an apprentice pharmacist in Aalborg, Jacob Paludan had met the young Eberlin when he was still a student attending upper secondary school; they had lodgings in the same boarding house, where they started a friendship that was to leave its imprint in the character of Otto.

Eberlin's family had a long tradition of legal and public service. His father was a police commissioner and later mayor of Thisted, which we have seen was the town on which Jacob Paludan modelled Havnstrup, Otto's childhood home. Eberlin initially studied law, but dropped out before finishing the course. He was a man of many talents; he drew and painted, for example, and even had work accepted for the annual Artists' Autumn Exhibition held at Den Frie Centre of Contemporary Art in Copenhagen.

One of Eberlin's many jobs in the US had been that of sign writer, and this led him into the advertising industry, a profession in which he continued to work with great success once he had returned to Denmark. In 1931 he was appointed head of department in Danske Erhvervs Annonce-Bureau (Advertsing Bureau for the Danish Chamber of Commerce), and the following year he set up his own business named Erik C. Eberlins Reklamebureau A/S, which grew to become one of the largest advertising agencies in Denmark. He later also achieved success as a magazine publisher with, for example,

"Mandens Blad" (a magazine about men's lives). This magazine, like other of Eberlin's projects, received financial support from Jacob Paludan.[195] And yet, Eberlin had a wild streak, which led him to lose ownership of his enterprises; in 1941 he got a job as business manager at Gigtforeningen (the Danish Rheumatism Association).

Eberlin could write, too, penning short stories, including crime stories, and two crime novels he had written were published posthumously. He and Jacob Paludan co-authored the stage play *Landet forude. Et spil om Utopien* (1928; The Country Ahead. A Play about Utopia).[196]

Jacob Paludan's Otto relies heavily on Eberlin, as Henrik Oldenburg points out when he notes: "As the pleasure-seeker and exploiter type, Otto bears a close likeness to Eric Eberlin".[197] It should here be said that Otto is completely his own man in terms of personality. And it must be stressed that Eberlin did not have Otto's criminal tendencies. But Oldenburg paints a detailed portrait of Eberlin, from which some fascinating similarities with Otto will be highlighted here.

Oldenburg tells us that Eberlin had no patience with the life of a law student in Copenhagen because the attendant poverty excluded him from expressing himself as the real man-of-the-world he so very much desired to be. He attempted to remedy his situation by selling collections of laws and pawning his textbooks! While he was a student he had worked at a law office and in a bank.

Eberlin spent bountifully when he was in the money, and for a while he lavished his largesse on an actress at a summer-season theatre. When funds were low he borrowed money from Jacob Paludan and others, in the firm belief that at some point he would again be a well-heeled man and able to repay the loan.

Eberlin had a taste for whisky and women, and he was married three times. When life in the fast lane got him down, he would easily fall into depression and pills, and he once went on such a comfort-eating binge that he put on 40 pounds in weight.

Three other 'testimonies' about Eberlin are informative for our understanding of Otto.

The first comes from a memoir essay written by Eberlin's second wife, Alice Scavenius (1904–2001),[198] in which she presents a colourful, in the best sense of that word, character sketch of Eberlin; for example: "He had all the virtues, and everyone loved him. He was pampered by one and all, and that is dangerous [...] when he turned on the charm, he was irresistible."[199]

The second interesting testimony that reveals Eberlin's significance as literary inspiration comes from the obituary written by one of his former employees, the editor Hartvig Andersen (1912–1968):

> He also had a god-given talent as a salesman [...] If persuasion was called for, he lacked neither doggedness nor willpower, and more than once he succeeded in cutting a deal that other mere mortals had thought impossible [...] How altogether characteristic it was that he preferred the cash payout to long-term interest. He was one of those people who are not made to wait. He demanded cash payment from life.[200]

The third testimony comes from the foreword to Eberlin's collection of short stories, *Americana* (1944), in which Jacob Paludan offers a sensitive characterisation of his late friend, from which this passage is taken:

> With his charm, his wit and his exceptional height, [he] invoked in his surroundings the idea that he was already a heavyweight – or at least one of the fortunate children of wealth who can do whatsoever they fancy [...] He was the man of every surprise and every opportunity, spontaneously gifted like no one else I have known. But he was, if one might express it thus, too tall to lie in the bed of reality.[201]

In 1943, divorced for the third time, deeply depressed and in debt, Eberlin committed suicide. Henrik Oldenburg and also Flemming Skipper[202] make much of Eberlin readily supplying material for Jacob Paludan's books by telling the author about his life, his childhood home in particular – the mayoral residence in Thisted, which would become the model for the governor's mansion in Havnstrup. Both analyses conclude that an actual agreement had been made, with Jacob Paludan paying for this 'service' by giving Eberlin money to fund his various projects. When Jacob Paludan found himself short of material he might even send a taxi to fetch his source. It is of course true that an author is at liberty to procure material in whatever manner he or she might see fit. The problematic aspect of Oldenburg's and Skipper's interpretations is that they see this practice as a manifestation of deficiency on Jacob Paludan's part; Oldenburg even writes: "On a number of occasions, Eric Eberlin supplied Paludan with material ('ideas') to make up for the latter's lack of imagination".[203]

The Otto-character builds on a variety of sources, but regardless of where the bricks have come from it is of course the way in which they are converted into a work of art that counts. Otto as finished product – impeccably constructed and original – lays the accusations against his imaginative creator to rest.

The Royal Oak

Jacob Paludan could have lived and worked as he pleased had not his lawyer cheated him out of the financial wherewithal to do so. Forced to make radical changes to his lifestyle, Jacob Paludan had decided to purchase Hestehaven and set up a poultry farm on the money he had left.

The lawyer involved proved to be a central inspiration to the fictional Otto, and without him Otto and indeed the novel *Jørgen Stein* would most likely never have been born. The lawyer despatched Jacob Paludan into a no-man's land where, although busy with his hens, he would surely have had the person responsible for his changed circumstances well and truly at the forefront of his mind. During this period, Jacob Paludan did no writing, and Otto could well have emerged from the intersection of literary withdrawal symptoms and thoughts of the conman lawyer.

Both in real-life and literary terms, this business with the lawyer undoubtedly conjured up the image of an 'Otto', which was then followed by the rest of *Jørgen Stein* – an interesting perspective.

The lawyer was called Kai Frederik von Linstow (1896–1929); in one of his letters, Jacob Paludan refers to the Hestehaven house as "Linstows Minde",[204] meaning 'Linstow's Memorial'! In an earlier letter, before he had detected the deceit, Jacob Paludan wrote of Linstow as his old friend and classmate, even boasting that he had enabled Linstow to start up his legal practice by standing surety for him.[205]

On 31.5.1929 *Politiken* newspaper reported that Linstow had disappeared from his home, and went on to follow the case day by day. In letters written at the time, Jacob Paludan's comments show that he monitored developments with great indignation.[206] Reading the newspaper over Jacob Paludan's shoulder is quite a harrowing thriller. We are present during the fertilization of the egg from which Otto was hatched.

So many details from *Politiken*'s coverage of the 'Linstow affair' have found their way into Jacob Paludan's account of Otto that either he must have cut the articles out or they had imprinted themselves into his memory. Jacob Paludan was of course already familiar with aspects of his old friend as described in the newspaper. The articles have a literary tone, which might also have appealed to Jacob Paludan, although it has to be admitted that the reporting might feel 'literary' when read with Otto in mind.

We will now follow *Politiken*'s coverage of the story, with a few abridgments and a few comments – although the extracts are actually unambiguous – and look at Jacob Paludan's reactions as recorded in his letters. On 31.5.1929, *Politiken* reported:

> The night before last, lawyer Kai Linstow failed to return to his home, and when he had still not appeared either there or at his office by yesterday morning, his family went to the police and requested they launch a search. The lawyer has of late been suffering from progressive diabetes, the dietary treatment of which he had difficulty in observing. It is therefore possible that he is wandering around in a poor state of health.
>
> Those close to him think it unlikely that he might have taken his own life. Up until his disappearance, he remained intensely interested in his business, which is in a period of intense growth, and his family circumstances are the very best.
>
> Yesterday evening we spoke with the lawyer's brother, administrative officer Linstow of the national police force, [who said]:
>
> 'He was feeling unwell six months ago, and a check-up revealed that he was suffering from severe diabetes. Nonetheless, this did not make him pay the necessary attention to his state of health [...] At times he was somewhat depressed, but when my eldest brother, who is head of section at his practice, spoke with him late in the evening before last, he noticed nothing unusual. The conversation mostly dealt with business matters. I can only imagine that he is wandering around unwell.'[207]

The article's denial of what the reader suspects is plain to read, and after reading the report Jacob Paludan himself concludes: "He has procured for me various securities, about the value of which I can but be suspicious [...] It is, however, still my unambiguous opinion that the man *is* honourable, but has simply been driven crazy by overwork [...]."[208]

The Royal Oak 91

The diabetes and Linstow's wandering are spelled out in the article, and it is not exactly surprising that he is intensely interested in his business, which had to be kept afloat, but to the very end he is capable of appearing unaffected by any problems when talking with his brother, even though this brother is on his staff. And a second brother is on the staff of the national police force – a Kafkaesque scenario.

On 1.6.1929, *Politiken* reported:

> The missing lawyer Linstow [...] is thought to have been seen in Ordrup last Thursday. At 9 o'clock on Thursday evening, leather-dealer Olsen, who has on numerous occasions received the lawyer in his home, sent his 16-year-old son, who is a bellboy at Cosmopolite Hotel, on an errand to fetch some pastries. The young man was accompanied by his 10-year-old brother. On the street called Hyldegaards Tværvej a large closed car drove towards the boys at high speed [...] 'That's Mr. Linstow, the lawyer,' said the bellboy to his brother, who was also certain it was him.
>
> Yesterday morning [...] they told what they had seen. Leather-dealer Olsen of course immediately notified the police [...].
>
> After this, there are no traces to be found. No one has seen the lawyer, an easily recognisable man. Speculation that he had gone to Gothenburg has not been corroborated.
>
> One line of enquiry being pursued is based on information about Mr. Linstow spending the Wednesday night at Palace Hotel. After his departure in the morning, the chambermaid had found blood stains, which might indicate that he had suffered a haemorrhage during the night. A 'diabetic' who does not take care of his diet, and has haemorrhages, will often become momentarily somewhat unbalanced.[209]

A man who is either wandering around or driving a large closed car at high speed is an alarming image of the 'on-the-run' phenomenon. The easily recognisable figure, and one who does not take care of his special diabetic diet, might indicate a substantial body weight. Here, too, the possibility of escape to Sweden is brought into the picture, and naturally an overnight stay at a good hotel, where the blood stains perhaps point ominously towards, yes, attempted suicide. It is also interesting to note that leather-dealer Olsen had received Linstow in his home on numerous occasions: the journalist rather clumsily intimates that Olsen has money at stake.

On 2.6.1929, *Politiken* reported:

> A Sad Conclusion to the Linstow Mystery. Lawyer found dead near Jægerspris.
>
> Lawyer Kai Linstow, who has been missing without trace since last Thursday morning, was yesterday found dead near Jægerspris. He had committed suicide by hanging himself from the 1,000-year-old Royal Oak tree.
>
> Around 4 o'clock, labourer Holger Olsen cycled [...] out to the Royal Oak tree, in the middle of the North Forest, where he saw lawyer Linstow's body. Olsen notified police officer Petersen in Jægerspris [...] officer Petersen [secured] the large number of business papers found in the dead man's pockets [...].
>
> Among the business papers were two letters: one to the deceased man's wife, and one to his brother, police administrative officer Linstow [...].
>
> Despite his infirmity, provisional results of the investigation show that Linstow had walked all the way out to the tree. Last Friday, therefore, he had been in Frederikssund without being recognised, even though the newspapers and radio had made his disappearance known far and wide. He must thus have conducted himself with the same composure by which he was characterised during his final conversations with his closest relatives here in Copenhagen.
>
> Lawyer Kai Linstow died just 33 years old. Despite his young age he had already acquired repute as a lawyer, and he was being entrusted with many big cases [...] All in all, the

office at no. 2 Ved Stranden, which he shared with the mayor, senior lawyer Godskesen, was full of business activity.

Finally, Linstow's name was very familiar at the trotting track; he owned a stable of 4 horses. He was a cheerful, enthusiastic man who made friends wherever he went. His wife and two children survive him.[210]

It is later revealed that up until two months before his suicide Linstow had worked for the above-mentioned Godskesen, who in *Jørgen Stein* is in all probability condensed into Goos, Otto's boss. The newspaper article presents a man considered by all to be a highly successful lawyer, a popular man who kept expensive trotting horses. This, too, paints a picture of composure and self-control as defence mechanism. We also see in Linstow, the missing man, a likely awareness of his extensive presence in the media. There is the onerous walk to the final scene, and the suicide note. The spectacular Royal Oak suicide is an illustration of reality as sometimes stranger than or too engineered for fiction, although of course Jacob Paludan would not want such a direct link to his novel.

The journalist elegantly includes the information that Linstow was found laden with business papers, which can be seen as an attempt both to preserve and conceal his activities.

Newspaper articles over the next couple of days, from 3.6. and 4.6.1929, reveal the background for the suicide. When commenting on the case in his letters, Jacob Paludan returns to the Royal Oak tree and the trotting horses:

> Yes, it was – it *was* a terrible parting shot, and I have not yet recovered. My old 'friend', classmate etc. etc. went off and hanged himself from the Royal Oak having, as my trusted advisor in financial matters and administrator of my money (and other people's) for 5 years, cheated and deceived in every conceivable way, and then left me, his family and many other people, to search through the ruins […] although I do not vex myself by working out what I could have bought for the

amount of money the fellow spent on keeping a stable of trotting horses.[211]

Politiken reports that Linstow had given hints in his suicide notes, and that a quick perusal of his business papers had caused the police to dive deeper into his financial dealings – in other words, the case 'snowballs'. It is also reported that the police are short on leads for their enquiries: "Nevertheless, the police have not received any requests from private individuals for further investigation",[212] but Jacob Paludan's name is mentioned as one of the individuals whose losses are to be assessed.

The newspaper article of 3.6.1929 also has new information about Linstow's movements in Jægerspris during the hours leading up to his suicide, and here Otto's final cup of coffee is served up on a silver platter:

> At around midnight he had turned up at a tenant farm in Dyrnæs, where at his request Mrs. Carlsen served him a cup of coffee. She has stated that he gave the impression of being very nervy. Sweat was dripping from his forehead and he was chatting incessantly. Among other things, he said that he was very familiar with the area, since he had spent a lot of time there as a child. He was now out to freshen-up those old impressions of the place. As he left she noticed that he was wobbly on his legs.[213]

Jacob Paludan endorses Linstow's choice of suicide rather than prison: "At this payment-due deadline he had the choice between the house of correction ('the cooler') or – the alternative, and he chose, not unwisely, the horrific way out."[214]

The letters reveal a particular sympathy for and a good deal of self-portrait in the naive Arthur Klein, Otto's main victim; Jacob Paludan writes: "I have, of course, been flagrantly neglectful in not keeping a more rigorous check […] my trust in people must gently be restored."[215] In this connection, it is delightful to learn from Henrik Oldenburg that Jacob Paludan later said he had actually questioned Linstow about his investments, but had let himself be fobbed off: "When Paludan periodically inquired about his money, he was told that it had been invested in real estate, and as proof he was taken out to Nørrebro and shown a couple of large apartment blocks. It later turned out that Paludan's money had never got that far."[216]

Linstow sends Jacob Paludan off to work in the countryside, where he revels in rural life for a good long while, writing that "every cloud has a silver lining".[217] The 'Linstow affair' certainly proved particularly advantageous for Danish literature.

Rounding off

We have seen how Jacob Paludan drew extensive material for Otto from two long-standing friendships; both Eric Eberlin and Kai Frederik von Linstow exercised a profound influence on the author's life. It is highly likely, however, that the outlines to Otto can be traced right back to the loneliness Jacob Paludan felt was the bedrock of his childhood home. This loneliness was the result of a pronounced absence of harmony in his relationship with his parents. The family imbalance had an offshoot in the favouritism the parents showed for their eldest son Hans Aage who, like Otto, was placed on a pedestal while Jacob Paludan was pushed to the sidelines. A career as a pharmacist was signposted along one of these sidetracks. Although pharmacy might have made Jacob Paludan think that any other way of earning a living, even a criminal one, was eminently preferable, it did actually take him off to the outside world, which furnished him with insights that might well have injected an international perspective into the issues in which Otto was embedded.

Jacob Paludan, circa 1965. Photograph: Herdis & Herman Jacobsen.

Epilogue

For many years *Jørgen Stein* has not been among the most read of Danish novels, to put it mildly, and second-hand copies have been readily and cheaply available. In *Aargangen der maatte snuble i Starten* (1943; The Generation that Could Not Help Stumbling at the Start), on the other hand, Ernst Frandsen wrote:

> Jacob Paludan is the most read of authors from the 1920s. One January day in 1942, I scoured the second-hand bookshops of Copenhagen without managing to find a single copy of any of his works. I received the same response everywhere I went, that a book written by Paludan is sold the same day it comes into the shop. Library lending registers tell a similar story.[218]

Interest in *Jørgen Stein* lasted into the 1950s, particularly among young people for whom it even surpassed central works of international literature as an identifier for their generation; in his introduction to the 2014 edition, Hans Hertel recalls:

> My generation was given *Jørgen Stein* as a confirmation gift, and I was ensnared, devoured Paludan's other books and quoted him in my essays. It was known as the 'senior-school bible', and it was just that; we 15–18-year-olds read until our copies fell apart. Surveys listed Paludan as senior-school pupils' favourite author – above Steinbeck, Hemingway and Remarque. This was due to the fact, I wrote in a very 17-year-old tribute on [Paludan's] 60th birthday in 1956, that

98   Epilogue

Jørgen Stein depicted the "complications, emotions and perceptions" of our age with such authenticity.[219]

The novel was a mirror on youth, writes Hans Hertel, adding that in the 1960s and 1970s this function was taken over by Leif Panduro's *Rend mig i traditionerne* (1958; *Kick Me in the Traditions*, 1961) and Klaus Rifbjerg's *Den kroniske uskyld* (1958; *Terminal Innocence*, 2015).[220] Hans Hertel identifies two other factors in the takeover: "modernism and the 1970s' critique of ideology demoted [Paludan's] novels".[221] In 1989 Danish cultural historian Martin Zerlang wrote that changes in mentality brought about by the youth counterculture rebellion finished off Jørgen:

> No, if the name Paludan is disappearing from the wider reading-world map, the cause is more likely that the 'youth psychology' (Rømhild), which defines the authorial territory, is not a landscape in which the modern youth soul can find habitation. Jørgen Stein with all his agonising frustrations was a mirror image for the older secondary school pupil; since the late 1960s, however, the older secondary school pupil's frustrations have mostly been a sphere of technical skill and fixed-term suffering.[222]

Whatever one might think about Jørgen, this affords him a certain status since it was the youth counterculture that finished him off! Can he be rediscovered, as Hans Hertel urges?[223] Perhaps he belongs in the sphere of the history of mentalities. Writing on the Danish public libraries' website, "Litteratursiden", when *Jørgen Stein* was re-published in 2014, Beth Høst asked: "Can young readers today take an interest in, or simply comprehend, the young Jørgen Stein's world [...] can Jørgen Stein's life and fate act as a mirror for a young person in the 21st century?" Beth Høst coaxes a response out of the young people by calling *Jørgen Stein* a magnificent example of a bildungsroman! And thus we are on the scent.

Epilogue **99**

I think it could be interesting to know what young people today think about Otto. Beth Høst sees this in him: "There is actually also a touch of modern television series in the depiction of Otto's fate (Jørgen's brother)." [224] Indeed, but why not pull him out of the parentheses with a feature film!

As Henrik Oldenburg points out, when the novel was originally published, a number of reviewers agreed that the portrait of Otto is in a class of its own.[225] Danish literary historian and critic Hans Brix (1870–1961) considered the depiction of Otto to be "a splendid little novel within the novel", adding "this is how a book should be written".[226] Tom Kristensen had fallen in love with Lily, and he saw the Lily-Otto couple as the central characters in the second half of the book: "These two underpin the tension in the novel for novel-technician Jacob Paludan",[227] and Paul la Cour was of the opinion that Otto's story "is convincing throughout, and its tragic conclusion is presented with great force".[228]

As we have seen, many other commentators have since highlighted the first-rate quality in the story of Otto. And yet, although a great deal has been written about Jørgen, Otto is only mentioned at random and briefly. One explanation for this imbalance is the tendency to see Otto as a masterly but also very simple or delimited characterisation serving a specific purpose. The approach taken by Danish literary historian and critic Sven Møller Kristensen (1909–1991) is typical of this stance. First, the singing of praise: "It is a vivid and dramatic illustration of post-war history. Otto is just as transparent a figure as Jørgen is veiled and intangible." Hand-in-hand with this praise, Sven Møller Kristensen stresses the one aspect *he* thinks is the reason for Otto's existence: "As a contrast to the idealistically searching Jørgen, his older brother Otto hits the buffers on pure materialism. He is a pleasure-seeker by nature."[229] Whereupon Sven Møller Kristensen continues to dig deeper into Jørgen.

The most comprehensive reading of Otto is the essay by Preben Erik Nielsen, views from which have been incorpo-

Epilogue

rated in the current analysis. The essay also contains a topicality 'update' from 1992 when Preben Erik Nielsen was managing director at the Danish branch of the Saatchi & Saatchi advertising agency:

> [*Jørgen Stein*] has been called the novel about a generation that could not help stumbling at the start, but today it would seem primarily to be a mirror of a time that in certain respects interestingly looks a lot like the 1980s we have recently put behind us, with phenomena such as failed business speculation, money fetishism and absence of coherence between money and morality.[230]

Preben Erik Nielsen then gets to the principal business in his topical updating, which is to highlight the following points of similarity with "the old story about Otto Stein":[231]

> At the time of writing, and in the specific context, three characters of our day surface, each in his way meeting the criteria of mentality and behaviour attributed to the business 'gambler': Johannes Petersen of Nordisk Fjer, Klaus Riskær Pedersen and Per Villum Hansen of Hafnia [...] They had to go all the way and walk on water before being exposed as false prophets [...] Their boards of directors were preoccupied with other matters, and had obviously not been conversant with essential aspects of the daily operations. The managing director had run the company as if it was his own, and forgotten that it was a responsibility on loan. The response to disastrous major investments has been new major investments, for which there has seldom been capital adequacy as a risk provision. 'Holes' have relentlessly been patched. Opaque and deficient balance sheets have been submitted [...] And when the curtain finally came down, it was suddenly clear to everyone that the situation was far worse than the worst imaginings.[232]

There has since been another financial crisis and a Danish 'gambler' who shares a name with Otto: Stein Bagger. He was CEO of the Danish software company known as IT Factory; charged with aggravated fraud and forgery, in 2009 he was sentenced to seven years in prison. Stein Bagger had been seen as a high-flier in the Danish business world – prior to the revelations. Towards the end of his essay, Preben Erik Nielsen makes it clear that he is absolutely not going for the Danish business community as a whole, which he sees as skilled and above-board. Even so, there can be no mistaking his intention given that the essay is an admonition to the entire spectrum of the business community: use the gambler cases as a guide to what you should *not* do. "Even the best families can have their 'bad apples',"[233] he writes. And Preben Erik Nielsen *has* seen the whole range of the 'Otto' figure, calling Otto "a modern man", and adding: "Every age produces its Otto Stein and its 'gamblers'."[234] And there is surely no harm in an admonition if it can heighten the influence of literature. Preben Erik Nielsen also mentions Herman Bang's *Stuk* (Stucco), and it is as if he is saying: avoid financial crises and fraud, read *Stuk* and *Jørgen Stein*.

The businessman's high estimation of Otto is shared by literary scholar Søren Schou, who in 1997 evaluates the scope of his story thus:

> The account of Otto's ever more desperate business dealings and delaying tactics, and his eventual suicide, still make for gruesome reading. With his finely-calibrated balance between tragedy and satire, this is a more powerful manifestation of the novel's critique of modern civilization than Jørgen's retreat to Havnstrup […] The musical-stylistic mastery he demonstrates in the depiction of '1920s yuppies' running amok in their pursuit of a pot of gold at the end of the rainbow will ensure *Jørgen Stein*'s status as a classic – long after the novel's positive counter-image has lost his radiance.[235]

Epilogue

The novel's topicality and status as a classic are embedded in Otto. It is in his story that the freshness of the picture is sustained. There are countless pieces to the Otto jigsaw, but Jacob Paludan has waved his magic wand over them and assembled an original whole. It is here that he shows his mastery as a storyteller.

I hope I have given Otto Stein the comprehensive reading he deserves. The approach to Jacob Paludan's other novels and his biography has been determined by this rationale, and hopefully 'Otto' has settled up by shedding new light on life and works.

An author's life should not be used as a key to the works, but is more than welcome as part of the picture in an entire creative process. Once dusted down, Jacob Paludan's life is in itself fascinating, and the elements that go into the moulding of Otto Stein are particularly informative for the study of the role of biography in the genesis of a work of art.

Notes

1 Foreword to: Paludan, *Jørgen Stein* (2014). (p. 11: "Ingen vil være i tvivl om, at de skildrede personer ligesom biler er 'samlede' af smådele, småiagttagelser tusinde steder fra." / [k]reativitetens magi). Jacob Paludan quote: *Aarhus Stiftstidende* newspaper, 23.06.1938.
2 Rifbjerg, *Nøleren*. (pp. 102–103: Nikolaj registrerede det alt sammen, og jeg overdriver ikke, hvis jeg siger, at når han tegnede en flyvemaskine, så var den mere flyvemaskine, end dem vi så i luften. Han kunne implantere en dødbringende fart i maskinen, en djævelsk aggressivitet, som rakte langt ud over normalen, og samtidig kunne han gå ud i det sivkransede område ned mod vandet og komme tilbage med en skitse af en sanger på et strå, der var så livagtig, at man kunne høre fuglen synge. Der var i det hele taget dette *mere* over alt, hvad han foretog sig.)
3 Sartre, *What is Literature?* pp. 29, 30, 33.
4 Paludan, *Jørgen Stein* (1966), pp. 626–627. (p. 558: Otto gik nogle Skridt frem, lige frem over Mosejorden. Et Skridt før han havde beregnet traadte han i det bundløse; det var, som om Skrækken blev nøjagtigt fordoblet derved. Vandet var bedøvende koldt. Maanestriben ude paa Søen fløj opad. Bobler og Brusen for Ørerne.)
All English-language quotations from the novel are from the 1966 translation by Carl Malmberg. All Danish passages and page numbers are taken from Paludan: *Jørgen Stein* (1948).
5 Jacob Paludan used the town of Thisted in north-western Jutland as his model for Havnstrup.
6 The Danish title *amtmand*: a senior administrative officer of a county, a district governor appointed by the Crown; the office was abolished after the 1970 local authority reform.
7 p. 31. (p. 33: Samtalen, der endnu gik i Bølger, vilde efter nogle Glas Vin gaa over i en vedholdende Buldren.)
8 p. 22. (p. 24: pille ved selve Vorherres Verdensorden.)

Notes

9   pp. 38–39. (p. 39: Gardinet løftede sig for et stærkt Vindpust, bugnede som et Sejl, og Lysflammerne vred sig som smaa Orme; Fru Nielsen trak de smukke Skuldre sammen med et kuldskært Skrig, som fik flere til at se forbavset op, og der blev pludselig et aldeles stille Sekund.)
10 p. 52. (p. 52: Jeg har ligesom ikke rigtig Magt over min Haand.)
11 Sørensen, "Jørgen Stein". (p. 48: Otto er en kalket grav, og hans afsluttende selvmord bliver en betydningsfuld markering af familien Steins forfaldshistorie, af dens manglende overlevelsesevne i den nye tid.)
12 Bang, *Håbløse slægter*. (p. 19: 'Der vil komme strenge tider', sagde Høg. Stella gav sig til at slukke lysene på buffeten ...)
13 Ibid. (pp. 22 and 23: Vinduet klaprede voldsomt imod muren. Vinden tog fat i gardinet og løsnede det, så det fløj som en fane langt ind i stuen; flammen i lampen slog op og osede ... / Vinduet brasede voldsomt mod muren, den ene rude gik itu, og skårene faldt raslende ned på stentrappen.)
14 Mann, *Buddenbrooks: The Decline of a Family*, p. 422.
15 Paludan, "Notater om Thomas Mann" (Notes on Thomas Mann). (p. 185: typisk Dødsroman, alle dens Linier peger nedad mod Forgængeligheden og Graven).
16 p. 6. (p. 9: hans Barndoms Legetøj).
17 p. 8. (p. 11: dette ubarmhjertige, bundløse Element).
18 p. 367. (p. 329: Set paa Krigens Baggrund syntes mange Aandsvidder, der før havde imponeret, temmelig smaa – som naar man vender Kikkerten om; Tonefald, man havde troet paa, blev hule, Fagter, der havde hypnotiseret, forekom naive.)
19 p. 8. (p. 10: at lukke sig smilende).
20 p. 5. (p. 8: hvid og ubevægelig som et kasseret Kravebryst.)
21 p. 377. (p. 337: som en søn).
22 Mann, *Buddenbrooks: The Decline of a Family*, p. 110.
23 Ibid., p. 517.
24 Ibid., p. 621.
25 Ibid., pp. 313–314.
26 Barfoed, "*Jørgen Stein* und Thomas Mann", p. 170. In this article, Niels Barfoed gives a general description of Jacob Paludan's interest in Thomas Mann and presents a number of interesting features shared by *Jørgen Stein* and, in particular, *Buddenbrooks: The Decline of a Family*, *The Magic Mountain* (1924, *Der*

Notes 105

Zauberberg), *Death in Venice* (1912, *Der Tod in Venedig*) and *Tonio Kröger* (1903).

27 p. 10. (p. 13: en dygtig og god ung Mand, hvem Fremtiden stod aaben. Aldrig havde man hos ham mærket uheldige Tilbøjeligheder).
28 p. 17. (p. 19: forudilende store Broder).
29 p.486. (p. 433: En Lykke er det dog, at det gaar Otto saa godt).
30 p. 59. (p. 59: Længe før man kunde se Havet viste Himlen dets Præg).
31 p. 18 and p. 19. (p. 20 and p. 21: solide hans Haandled allerede var [...] Laarene, der fyldte Tøjet til sidste Millimeter.)
32 p. 20. (pp. 22–23: Hans psykologiske Sans var ikke særlig udviklet, men han opfattede dog elementære Misstemninger.) / p. 375. (p. 336: en tung Natur [...] tykke Hudpanser [...] indviklede Grublerier over sin Sjæls Beskaffenhed).
33 Frederiksen, *Jacob Paludan*, p. 56. (åndelig højde [...] et pund dumhed i panden).
34 Schou, "Provins og apokalypse. Jacob Paludan: *Jørgen Stein*" (Province and Apocalypse. Jacob Paludan: *Jørgen Stein*). (pp. 228–229: falsk loyalitet, der lige netop antyder den underliggende sarkasme). To illustrate this narratorial function, Søren Schou refers to the following passage in *Jørgen Stein*, p. 489: 'We lawyers have a somewhat doubtful reputation,' Otto muttered with the sadness of one who has been maligned. (p. 436: "Vi har jo et noget blandet Ry blandt Folk," mumlede Otto med en med Urette beklikket Stands sørgmodige Misantropi.) Søren Schou is making the point that here Otto is revealed to imagine that his profession as lawyer is unjustly the object of public contempt – precisely what it is *not* in the novel.
35 Ibid. (p. 229: fløjlshandsken trækkes af jernnæven / særdeles kontant satiriker).
36 Mikhail Bakhtin describes this feature of Dostoevsky's work as 'polyphony'; see: Bakhtin, *Problems of Dostoevsky's Poetics*.
37 Paludan, "Den unge Dostojefski" (The Young Dostoevsky). (pp. 82–83: At han kendte Lasten som en Virkelighed og ikke blot som en Skrivebordsanstrengelse, giver ham det Privilegium, at de mindre frelste i ham fornemmer én, som kender dem [...] Dostojefski er for dem, der som Goethe har mærket Spiren til alt muligt i sig, ikke for det absolut plet- og støvfrie Citydress.)
38 p. 411. (p. 367: "Ikke for langt," bad Otto, da Hr. Hambro førte

dem et Stykke Vej ind i Storskoven for at vise dem Vandmosen. Det var en lille, stille Sø i Skovensomheden, indfattet i en Mur af Graner og af Birke, hvis slørlette Løvbræmmer netop nu var af stor Virkning som Kontrast. I Tavshed saa de ud over det blanke Vand, der syntes at have indsuget Vinternætternes Mørke og at gemme det Sommeren over. / "Uf," sagde Eva pludselig. / Ottos alvorlige Blik vendte sig fra Søen mod hende.)

39 Joyce, *Ulysses*, p. 208.
40 p. 491 and p. 184. (p. 437: blomsterslank; p. 168: som tynde, duftende Blomsterblade).
41 p. 474. (p. 422: en yndig Dame, hvis Fader gennemfløj Landene, stoppet med Patenter, som et økonomisk Projektil.)
42 p. 175. (p. 161: Noget fremmedartet, ubestemmeligt var der ved hende, ofte virkede hun kun som en stor Backfisch, men i visse Belysninger kunde hendes Ansigt og hendes Pande have en Genspejling af stor Alder og bundløs Erfaring.)
43 Zerlang and Reinvaldt, "Man kan ikke male ud over rammen. Om klassebevidsthed og karakterstruktur i Jacob Paludans *Jørgen Stein*" (You Cannot Paint Beyond the Frame. On class consciousness and character structure in Jacob Paludan's *Jørgen Stein*). (p. 200: Den udvidelse af forlystelseslivet (barer, biografer, natklubber osv.), som tyvernes produktionsforøgelse giver anledning til, rykker seksualiteten bort fra intimsfæren. Denne udvikling . . . tematiseres især med Ottos og Lilys forhold.)
44 Kehler, *Paa Jagt efter Geniet* (Pursuing the Genius). (p. 108: Har man levet i Danmark og København, har man også truffet Otto Stein og fru Lily.)
45 p. 380. (p. 340: Hvor forbandet, at man ikke kunde jage sin Haand ud i den sikre, rundelige Fremtid og skrabe en Forsyning Dalere tilbage til den magre Nutid!)
46 p. 263. (p. 235: Hvorfor skal de unge savne og de gamle mæske sig? Vi maa bryde os Vej, og én maa gøre Begyndelsen.)
47 Fitzgerald, *The Great Gatsby*, p. 105 and p. 106.
48 pp. 181–182. (p. 166: kunne træde hen til ethvert Bord og byde Forfriskninger over hele Linien, uden at noget saa lurvet som Betænkeligheder ved Omkostninger skulde lamme den Haand, der følte sig skabt til den brede Gestus.)
49 p. 362. (p. 324: Det er Kapitalen, der bestemmer her i Verden, ikke Alderdommen).
50 Frederiksen, *Jacob Paludan*. (p. 55: denne antikke visdom).

51 p. 388. (p. 347: det grusomme, absolutte Spil, der ikke spurgte om Skæbner, Lykke, Liv eller Død, men havde sit eget Forløb: Omsætningen.)
52 Zerlang and Reinvaldt, "Man kan ikke male ud over rammen". (p. 158: Hans selvmord . . . er den endelige bekræftelse på, at han har druknet sin personlighed i omsætningens bølger.)
53 In 1918, DKK 400 would correspond to a January 2021 value of approximately DKK 13,000 / EUR 1,750 /USD 2,100 / GBP 1,550.
54 p. 383. (342: et hændeligt Uheld i en stor forretning.) / p. 392. (p. 351: Driftslaan).
55 p. 474. (p. 422: Otto lugtede Bo.)
56 In 1923, DKK 70,000 would correspond to a January 2021 value of approximately: DKK 2,123,000 / EUR 285,000 / USD 346,000 / GBP 253,000.
57 p. 487. (p. 434: en værdig Idiot.)
58 p. 489. (p. 435: Med let skælvende Hænder optalte han ved Banklugen de 140 Femhundredkronesedler – fjorten Bundter med ti i hver. Personalets og Kundernes Øjne hvilede uvilkaarligt paa ham under dette, og han sørgede for at tale uanfægtet: "Og saa sætter vi dem ind paa en Bankbog til i Morgen." Sikken Flothed, tænkte Klein overvældet, en hel Bankbog for en Dag! Hans Fader havde været Aar om at slide en Bankbog op.)
59 p. 489. (p. 436: Stumper af Begravelseshymner og en ældgammel Revyvise). / p. 490. (p. 437: Kram, hvad? Og lutter solide Lejere.) / p. 489. (p. 436: Man er vel nok Finansmand).
60 p. 375. (p. 335: vilde staa midt i Velstandsstrømmen og grave sindrige Sidekanaler for den, naar den skiftede Leje).
61 p. 523. (p. 467: Men det gik, om end sommetider som hos Tryllekunstneren: pludselig er der ingenting under den høje Hat, og ligesaa pludselig er der noget igen. Det gjaldt blot at være over det selv, hele Tiden, og med Tryllestaven dirigere de vandrende Pengebeløb, saa de altid var dér, hvor et Ansigt begyndte at vise den første Panderynke.)
62 p. 596. (p. 532: Skyskraberforretninger).
63 p. 523. (p. 467: Otto traadte Æggedansen.)
64 Nielsen, "Den store spiller" (The Big Player), article in *Politiken* newspaper, 27.7.1992. (Det er en rigtig 'gambler-historie', om en mand, der er villig til at sætte alt på spil i 20'ernes casinoøkonomi.) / (Mange husker Dostojevskijs rystende lille roman

om roulettespilleren, der sætter sin sjæl på spil i endeløse livtag med hjulet og den lille kugle, for at ende som et desperat menneske, der er parat til at gå planken ud for sin store tanke – ideen om det ultimative system, der vil eliminere alle tilfældigheder, sprænge banken og selvfølgelig resulterer i den helt store gevinst.)

65 Ibid., from: Anna Dostoevsky: *Dostoevsky: Reminiscences*, Liveright Paperback 1975 / 1977, pp. 131–132.

66 p. 107. (p. 101: "Ja, paa Ære," sagde Jørgen dystert, og mindedes i Tobaksrøgen og det sene, natlige Lampelys en russisk Roman om desperate, men ærekære Eksistenser og en Roulette.)

67 p. 606. (p. 541: Naturligvis, saa vilde Helvede være løs i Morgen, men hvor var man i Morgen […] der var endnu Tid til Overvejelser.)

68 p. 378. (p. 338: Fra Sydvinduerne kunde man et Stykke tilbage i Gaden se en beslægtet Virksomhed, Sagfører Tollers; men her var ingen Vildvin, ingen ny Maling; Vinduerne syntes støvede, et stadigt Halvmørke maatte herske derinde. Naar Otto kiggede derover, følte han sig i høj Grad paa Lyssiden og priste sin Lykke.)

69 p. 601. (p. 537: [e]n ren Satan […] en ren Edderkop […] sukkerlysten Spyflue).

70 Dostoevsky, *Crime and Punishment*, p. 301.

71 p. 605. (p. 540: Gudbevares, kære Kollega, en saa – fængslende og kendt Mand i Byens Liv maa virkelig interessere – psykologisk og paa flere Maader. / Vil De ryge? Tobak beroliger, man kan næsten glemme Morgendagen over en god Cigar. Morgendagen, ak, ja.)

72 In his review of the Danish edition of this book, Danish literary historian Johnny Kondrup highlights this revenge motif, for which I thank him by pointing it out here. The review is in: *Danske Studier* (Danish Studies), 2019, pp. 275–278.

73 p. 374. (p. 335: Otto Stein lagde sig ud. Det var, som om hans Legeme foruddiskonterede den Velstand, der var hans Maal.)

74 Lundbo, *Jacob Paludan*. (pp. 102–103: graadige Materialisme).

75 Bondebjerg, "Borgerlig individualisme i havsnød" (Bourgeois Individualism in Distress). (p. 375: et fedt og oppustet symbol for den usunde, spekulative kapitalisme).

76 Schou, "Provins og apokalypse. Jacob Paludan: *Jørgen Stein*". (p. 229: forvandles til et kødbjerg med få menneskelignende træk

i behold / p. 228: fortæller om en verden i færd med at ødelægge det menneskelige).
77 Zerlang and Reinvaldt, "Man kan ikke male ud over rammen". (p. 183: grænseløse æderi [...] incestuøs regression / p. 184: skaffe sig den moderlige omsorg i oralt regi). In her article "Jørgen Stein", Marianne Sørensen calls Otto's meals "regressive eating orgies". (p. 49: regressive spiseorgier).
78 p. 586. (p. 523: Men overdaadig Mad giver Kardialgi. Hele Formiddagen er det, som en Sugekop har sat sig fast paa Underlivet. Spyttet smager syrligt, og man kunne tænke sig at kaste op. Men det hjælper, naar man straks begynder at fylde paa igen.) With thanks to Søren Schou for bringing my attention to the issues around heartburn.
79 Mann, *Buddenbrooks: The Decline of a Family*, p. 94.
80 Bang, *Stuk*. (p. 304: den stjaalne og falske Mønt).
81 Ibid. (p. 258: Hver Dag fordrede jo Udveje).
82 Ibid. (p. 45: Der er jo ingen Provinser mere [...] Der er jo kun ét eneste stort København, det hele ...)
83 Nielsen, "Den store spiller" (The Big Player). (Hjernen har arbejdet dag og nat i årevis, og sekundviseren accelererer sin nedtælling mod nul).
84 Lundbo, *Jacob Paludan*. (p. 103: selvmedlidende).
85 p. 603. (p. 538: Denne ene Tanke: at han var et rigt udstyret Menneske, kunde han ikke give til Pris.)
86 Blixen, *Seven Gothic Tales*, pp. 171–172.
87 p. 618. (p. 551: Otto følte sig lettet; endnu var Samfundet og han gode Venner, han var Genstand for dets huldsalige Omsorg.)
88 p. 610. (p. 544: Begge var i graat og af ubestemmeligt Ydre [...] et Par Herrer med god Tid). / p. 611. (p. 545: Var det Sporhaner, eller bildte han sig det ind?) / p. 610. (p. 544: Det var som om de langsomt trængte sig frem til Tydelighed indenfor hans Horisont). / p. 626. (p. 558: Endnu en Bil passerede, og det syntes ham, at den sagtnede Farten.)
89 p. 614. (p. 548: Sengen var saa kold, at han kom til at ryste og klapre [...] den uformelige Dyne skimtedes i Mørket som et Isbjerg.)
90 p. 615. (p. 548: tænk, blot det at fodre Høns og Duer, i Haarløv. Det var underligt.)
91 p. 603. (p. 538: Politiet, Cellen, Retten, Straffen.)
92 pp. 615–616. (p. 549: Vejene var nyfrosne og krævede

110 *Notes*

Forsigtighed. Han kom til at tænke over dette: hvorfor være forsigtig? Jo, fordi netop en Ulykke vilde lukke En hjælpeløst ind i Fælden. Han vilde blive plejet med yderste Omhu for at kunne blive overgivet til Politiet i god, frisk Kondition –).

93 Hansen, "Djævleblændt teologi. Livskraft og tilgivelse i Dostojevskijs 'store' romaner" (Consummate Theology. Vitality and forgiveness in Dostoevsky's 'major' novels), *Bogens Verden*, no. 3, 2005.

94 Paludan, *Birds Around the Light* (1928), pp. 271–272. (p. 187: De lange Timer derinde forhærder. Fængselet renser ikke for de Forbrydertanker, der fandtes, men bereder Jordbunden for dem dér, hvor de ikke fandtes. Fangen er melankolsk, naar han kommer, men hadefuld, naar han gaar. Man taler i denne Forbindelse om Forbedringshuse.)
All English-language quotations from the novel are from the 1928 translation by Grace Isabel Colbron. All Danish passages and page numbers are taken from Paludan: *Fugle omkring Fyret* (1927).

95 Larsen, *Alberti-Katastrofen*. (pp. 158 and 159: Da Alberti ankom til Horsens den 20. december 1910, blev det noteret i hans nyoprettede stambog, at han var 188 cm høj, vejede 138½ kg, og havde en livvidde på 155 cm. Fængslet var ikke vant til indsatte af det format, så man måtte sy en særlig dragt til ham […] I sommeren 1912 var hans vægt nede på 71 kilo. Han var næsten holdt op med at spise, var blevet apatisk, og man frygtede for hans liv.) Henrik Larsen also writes about Alberti's brother Carl, who had trained as a pharmacist and then settled in Argentina, where he committed suicide in 1893; in his time, Carl had been suspected of committing fraud.

96 Jacob Paludan had possibly also taken note that Alberti's predecessor as Minister of Justice was called August Herman Ferdinand Carl <u>Goos</u>.

97 Larsen, *Alberti-Katastrofen*, pp. 183–184.

98 p. 625. (p. 557: en Kop af et flere Gange opvarmet Bryg.) / p. 626. (p. 558: skulde jo snart se til at faa lukket.) / p. 625. (p. 557: Det var sent, han kom, mente Konen.) / p. 624. (p. 556: der endnu var Lys.) / p. 626. (p. 558: han følte med sig selv, at hvis der blev budt ham en Seng, saa vilde han i Guds Navn glemme, at han var en Stein, og tage hele Historien – Arrestation, Dom og Straf. Det andet, det var dog saa—saa. Der var intet Ord, der kunde omspænde, hvordan det var.) / p. 626. (p. 558: Otto

Notes 111

betalte og sagde Farvel med grødet Stemme. Den sidste Haand havde trukket sig tilbage.)

99 Paludan, "I det skraa, øjenblændende Sollys" (In the Oblique, Dazzling Sunlight). (p. 46: Forbi bliver alting, ogsaa alle Ture og deres elysiske Højdepunkter, og lad det blot ske, naar der stadig kan regnes med Mulighed for een Gang til.)

100 Dostoevsky, *Crime and Punishment*, p. 163. As his time is about to run out, Svidrigailov extols life by expressing great annoyance at his feverish state; he would rather have shot himself when in a good healthy condition.

101 In his review of the Danish edition of this book, Martin Zerlang suggests looking at Otto's conman character in relation to René Girard's theory of mimetic desire. The suggestion is herewith taken on board – with thanks. Martin Zerlang's review is published in "Scandinavian Studies", Vol. 92, No. 2, 2020, University of Illinois Press. The following books by René Girard have been consulted for this section: *Deceit, Desire & the Novel*, The John Hopkins University Press 1965 /1976; *Violence and the Sacred*, Bloomsbury Academic 1988/ 2013. The following Danish studies of René Girard's theories have been consulted: Hans J. Lundager Jensen, *René Girard*, Anis 1991; Finn Frandsen, "Begæret, volden og offeret" (The Desire, the Violence and the Victim), Religionsvidenskabeligt Tidsskrift 6, 1985.

102 p. 632. (p. 563: Men saa kom da Dagen, da Otto ude paa Bispebjerg blev forvandlet til den Kalk og Magnesia, der er saa langt modstandsdygtigere end Menneskets Karakter).

103 p. 631. (p. 563: De døde rider hurtigt, men Otto red paafaldende hurtigt. Hans personlige Træk opløstes, blot man saa på dem i Tanken).

104 Mai and Dalager, *Litteraturteori og analysestrategi* (Literary Theory and Analytic Strategy). (p. 85: en virkelig levende person). The authors explain that Otto comes alive "because he is depicted with various contradictions and nuances, and because the reader follows Otto's development in a specific trajectory with a packed storyline". (p. 85: fordi han skildres med forskellige modsigelser og nuancer, og fordi læseren oplever Otto's udvikling i et konkret handlingsmættet forløb). Of Otto's overall story, they write that it is "a particularly significant plot thread, the most concise in the novel". (p. 81: en særdeles vigtig handlingssekvens, der fremtræder som romanens mest koncise).

105 p. 637. (p. 567: i Leifs Sind var der tunge Vægte, der trak nedad, en sær Egenvilje til Ødelæggelse.)
106 p. 648. (p. 577: Han fandt en Notits om Otto – 'den dygtige unge Landsretssagfører'... Det var som at slaa tilbage i en uskyldigere Verden / selve Tiden igennem ham som en susende Vind).
107 p. 294. (p. 263: Hvor hendes Kind var brændende varm, og hvor hendes Legeme skælvede! At tage om hende var som at stikke Haanden ned i Halm og finde varme smaa Hundehvalpe frem.)
108 p. 303. (pp. 271–272: Det var for Leif ganske i Traad med den Tilværelsens djævelske Taktik, der altid fører de forkerte sammen med de forkerte, at hendes Ansigt ved Farvellet blev mildt som Sødgrød med Smørhul i).
109 p. 693. (p. 617: Deres Forundringsudbrud krydsedes) / p. 206. (p. 187: dobbelt hvidt og langthenlysende).
110 p. 29. (p. 31: Dobbelthage hvilede blødt over Flippen, som en Dyne over en Tøjsnor.)
111 p. 25. (p. 27: Berg, en Blok af Forspisthed med et blodappelsinrødt Ansigt).
112 p. 41. (p. 42: dampede levende langs Glassets Sider og smagte som stærkt Solskin.)
113 p. 177. (p. 163: en brun Likør groede som en Blomst paa Dugen.)
114 p. 305. (p. 274: *come on* og *hurry up*-Humør) / p. 275. (p. 246: endogsaa hans Hvile i Stolen syntes præget af Tempo.) / p. 308. (p. 276: Elektrikeren var morgenfrisk hele Dagen).
115 Barfoed, "Pietetens helvede. Jacob Paludans *Jørgen Stein*" (The Hell that is Respect, Jacob Paludan's *Jørgen Stein*). (p. 44: det episke liv / en skæbne, omend den fører i hundene).
116 Skou-Hansen, "Forsvar for prosaen" (In Defence of Prose), pp. 138–139.
117 la Cour, review of *Jørgen Stein*. (pp. 346–347: Otto repræsenterer Slægtens økonomiske, Jørgen dens kulturelle Fallit).
118 Frandsen, *Aargangen der maatte snuble i Starten* (The Generation that Could Not Help Stumbling at the Start). (p. 52: Paa Ottos historie har Forfatteren anvendt hele sin Dygtighed i Arrangementet, Kracket og Faldet er klassisk Handlingsroman uden Skelen til Billige Effekter.)
119 As mentioned in the Preface, this chapter is a presentation of Jacob Paludan's five novels leading up to *Jørgen Stein*, with the specific purpose of showing elements that paved the way for Otto.

120 Paludan, *De vestlige Veje* (1922; The Western Roads). (p. 27: Harry rejste sig langsomt og gik hen i Døren. Sletten laa blaagrøn udenfor i den faldende Sol. Længe saa han ud i den store Ensomhed. Ensomheden, der lukker sig efter den, der springer ud deri, uden en Boble, uden en Ring.)

121 Ibid. (p. 39: Naar de nævnte ordet Dollars, fik de samme Udtryk i deres Øjne, som en Katolik faar, naar han nævner Jomfru Maria.)

122 Ibid. (p. 39: Arbejdsmenneskets Sum bliver først rund, naar Livsdagene er blevet det, naar Handel og Had for evig hører op.)

123 Ibid. (p. 46: I Selenien [...] arbejder man, til man svimler, for at skabe et Økonomisk Grundlag for Villaen og Limousinen. Her ødes de Bedste Aar, for at man kan byde over Livets Glæder, naar man ikke mere kan nyde dem.)

124 Ibid. (p. 58: det uopnaaelige bliver det eneste, der er værd at eje [...] Maanen er det, vi vil have).

125 Ibid. (p. 69: Paa tredje Avenue bor Pantelaanerne saa tæt som Mider i en Ost.)

126 Ibid. (p. 74: Er man ikke hensynsløs og brutal her, saa gaar man tilbunds.)

127 Ibid. (pp. 76–77: En lille Kontraktion i Pengemarkedet er nok til at sende Tusinder af arbejdsløse paa Gaden . . . Hvert syvende Aar sker Katastrofen: Folk bliver som vilde Dyr, gaar ind i Forretningerne og tilbyder at arbejde for det halve af, hvad de allerede ansatte faar. En behændig Operation, der bringer Pengenes Købeevne i Vejret. Hvem tjente?)

128 Erich Maria Remarque, *Im Westen nichts Neues*, translated by Arthur Wesley Wheen, Little, Brown and Company, 1929.

129 Paludan, *Søgelys* (1923; Searchlight). (pp. 123–124: "Ved De [...] hvordan Giftgas er?" Han maatte tale: "Det er en brun Taage, som lægger sig langsomt og begynder at kvæle. Den ligger paa Maven over Slagmarken og har ganske god Tid, efterhaanden faar den Fingrene ned i Skyttegravenes Kamre, den har ti Tusind Fingre med skarpe Negle! Folk tumler frem mod den, saa jager den en Negl ned i Lungerne [...] Man har ogsaa Sennepsgranater. De falder i en Klynge Mænd, der staar og taler om Middagsmad og laver Brandere. Saa siger den whuzz! Og Mændene farer rundt og brøler, med Ild over hele Kroppen og blinde og døve skriger de op som Grise [...].")

130 Ibid. (p. 75: Eksplosioner i Hjernen).

114 Notes

131 Ibid. (p. 80: en lille Frist [...], nogle Solopgange, nogle Gader med Mennesker i. / p. 83: Kødet, der uopfordret og paa egen Haand stejlede overfor Udslettelsen.)
132 Ibid. (p. 169: Det var blot at gaa ned ad Trappen og videre ud paa det hvide Gulv, ud mod Bøjerne, der som skraatstillede Koste stak op gennem Isen, videre, til det knirkede, videre til det brast. En Isflage løfter sig, han glider og forsvinder. Laaget lukkes tæt og nøjagtigt. Nat og Øde, intet er sket. Og saa – lang Tavshed, uendeligt boblende Mørke [...].)
133 Ibid. (pp. 169–170: Han [...] saa paa det nederste Trin, paa noget mærkeligt. Ikke andet end en selvdød Fisk, der var skyllet op [...]. / p. 171: frygtløs saa han frem i Mørket. / p. 172: blinkede Lys imod ham fra en lille Kafé).
134 Jacob Paludan, *Jørgen Stein*, p. 624 (p. 556: lille Traktørsted, hvor der endnu var Lys.)
135 Jacob Paludan, *Søgelys*. (p. 175: den korteste Vej til Politiet.)
136 Ibid. (p. 8: Skum paa Overfladen.)
137 Ibid. (p. 151: saa tom som et udblæst Æg.)
138 Ibid. (p. 14: saa ukendt af alle, som havde det aldrig eksisteret. / vi maa købe dig løs, gamle Ven).
139 Vejstrand: 'vej' meaning 'road' or 'way'; 'strand' meaning 'beach', 'shore' and also 'to be stranded', 'to founder'.
140 Paludan, *En Vinter lang* (1924; Winter Long). (p. 5: al Sol gaar iglemme.)
141 Ibid. (p. 105: Livets velvillige Magter.)
142 Ibid. (p. 117: Han gik fra det golde Stadium til det frugtbare [...] alt syntes at byde ham velkommen [...] det var godt at naa frem til at kunne kalde noget for sit, naar man har været Turist i en Menneskealder).
143 *The Liar*, p. 179. *Løgneren*, 1950. (p. 141: være Efterkrigstidsmenneske og finde alt meningsløst).
144 Ibid., p. 153 (p. 119: Jeg var en Tid, et helt Aar, i den syvende Himmel, for det var altsaa Birte og mig, og tilmed studerede jeg Litteratur).
145 Ibid., pp. 194 and 198 (pp. 153 and 157: Det var første Gang man stod her paa Nærbjerg og vidste, at til denne Jordbanke i Søen var for altid ens Skæbne bundet [...] man er ikke mere en Person på Besøg, men en Mand paa sin Plads.)
146 Ernst Frandsen identifies inspiration from Knut Hamsun's character Johan Nilsen Nagel in *Mysterier* (1892; *Mysteries*, various

Notes 115

translations), in Frandsen: *Aargangen der maatte snuble i Starten* (The Generation that Could Not Help Stumbling at the Start), p. 33.
147 Paludan, *Birds Around the Light* (1928), p. 88. (p. 62: Liv er Risiko.)
148 Ibid., p. 237. (p. 164: Mammon havde været Præst, da de gik til Alteret.)
149 Ibid., pp. 79-80. (p. 57: Naar han om Aftenen paa Cafe lod sig række Pelsen og den høje Hat, mens han med et indknebent Øje tændte Cigaretten, plejede al Støj og Samtale at dæmpes ved Bordene. Hans Garderobe, hans vaner, intet Stof var uudtømmeligere.)
150 Ibid., p. 234. (p. 161: Hans Ansigt fortalte, at han kendte alle de Livets Glæder, der købes med Helbred.)
151 Ibid., pp. 291-292. (pp. 200-201: Dog, det hele skyldtes jo kun et Sammentræf af uheldige Omstændigheder. Indvielsen herude og den paafølgende Sanering af Sandhavns Økonomi vilde forandre alt; hvem vidste, maaske var de første Købere til hans Grunde allerede paa Trapperne.)
152 Ibid., p. 257. (p. 177: Foryngelsens vilde, krydrede Urt).
153 Ibid., p. 321. (p. 219: Langsomt aabnede hun sine Øjne og saa hans Ansigt – en svagt graa, vablet Masse.)
154 Ibid., pp. 322-323. (p. 220: i fuld Dress.)
155 Jacob Paludan: *Markerne modnes* (1927), Steen Hasselbalchs Forlag 1962 (p. 74: Lærer du aldrig at tage selv, saa vil andre tage fra dig, Ivar.)
156 Ibid. (p. 144: en ny og frigjort Tids Datter […] at Livet skal Nydes, før det visner.)
157 Ibid. (p. 122: slog hun sin Arm om hans Skulder. Ivar sad ganske stille; ingen Fugl under en Haand kunde have siddet mere dødstille.)
158 Ibid. (p. 70: knirkende indre Trappe […] hun lagde Armen om Bettinas Liv og glædede sig til rigtig at kysse hende på Vejen derop […]De unge Piger kom ned, røde og leende).
159 Ibid. (p. 216: Saa gik hun efter ham, og i den mørke Gang, lige udenfor Soveværelset, greb hun om ham, hendes Mund gled over hans, og man hørte en stiv Hat rulle over Gulvet.)
160 Ibid. (pp. 40-41: Det var kommet saa pludseligt, skønt han længe havde maattet sukke, naar han forestillede sig hendes lyseblaa, tørstige Øjne, og blade i Poesibøger. Hendes Nærhed havde gjort

ham urolig; det var som en Sommervarme, naar han vidste hende bag sig. Med ét mærkede han hendes Ildkys i sin Nakke; hun drog ham til sig, tættere, tættere; han havde ikke vidst, at man kunne komme hinanden saa nær, men hun havde sin leende og sukkende Viden. Det var en Maaned siden. Endnu i Nat havde han været hos hende, fra Midnat til henad Morgen; hun havde kaldt ham – alt muligt, som en Lavastrøm ind i hans Øre, og hendes smalle Seng havde været som en Rist fuld af Gløder.)

161 Ibid. (p. 218: I Dag vidste Ivar, at han i Kærlighed kun havde faaet, hvad Ralf havde vraget.)

162 Ibid. (p. 220: Hun løb lige mod Rørmosen, der skjulte sit sorte Vand bag en Jordkam. Hun kunne falde i; han maatte standse denne Forfølgelse. Da han stod stille, saa' han sig om; nej, ingen iagttog dem. Han saa' frem paany. Hun var der ikke. Hun maatte være gledet i Vandet. Hans Hjerte begyndte at slaa højt, nogle forfærdelige Slag med lange Mellemrum. Han stirrede anspændt frem mod den mørke, lige Vold af Jord. Hvorfor raabte hun ikke? Den mindste Lyd vilde forvandle ham fra en Saltstøtte til et Menneske, der sprang til Hjælp . . . Da saa' Ivar, skarpt tegnet mod Himlen, en tynd Arm stikke sig op, fægte og gribe for sig. Intet andet, og ikke en Lyd. Han syntes, Armen truede, hans Mund aabnede sig. Knæene svigtede, han faldt. Derved fik han Øje paa, hvad han havde i Haanden: Pulveret. Han rev febrilsk Kapslen op og indsnusede dens Indhold . . . Roligt saa' han frem mod Mosen, hvor der nu intet var at se, hvor Vandet nu maatte have lukket sig og gjort sin barmhjertige Gerning . . . han rejste sig fri og lykkelig.)

163 Ibid. (p. 250: Der begyndte at komme Fedt hist og her, ogsaa ned over Kinderne. Og hans Flipper blev stadig for smaa. Men hvor lavede hun ogsaa god Mad, Fru Børgesen. Den forlorne Skildpadde og den Æblekage, man fik det simpelthen ikke bedre nogetsteds . . . Hun var jo nok lidt svær og almindelig, men havde varme Øjne . . . jaja, saa blev det vel hende.)

164 Ibid. (p. 249: en gul Flaske).

165 Paludan, *De vestlige Veje*. (pp. 54–55: Vildmosen er et Plateau af fugtige Jordvolde, der omgærder Bassiner med gurglende Vand. Sæt ikke Deres Fod der [...] Mennesker vilde blive suget ned uden Skaansel. Tænk Dem, at De staar derude! De vilde raabe op, men ingen hører det [...] Nu naar Mudderet Dem til Brystet, det er koldt og slimet; De presser imod, men man kan ikke træde

Vande i Dejg. De har blot to Minutter igen, til religiøse Overvejelser . . . [...] Saa, nu fylder Mudderet Næse og Mund; Tavshed. Længe efter at Deres Hoved er borte, rager en Arm i Vejret [...] og Fingrene forsvinder, med et tilfreds Kluk sletter Vandet ud efter Dem.) In the first edition of *De vestlige Veje*, Petri is called Jacoby.
166 Paludan, *Markerne modnes*. (p. 59: hans litterære Force var Dødsscener).
167 Paludan, "Ved Overtagelsen af en jysk Hytte" (On Taking Over a Cabin in Jutland).
168 Ibid. (p. 64: udenfor de virksommes Arealer).
169 The job title of *herredsskriver*: an old title for a public official in a law court serving a jurisdiction district.
170 Oldenburg, *Historien om et venskab* (The Story of a Friendship). (p. 16: undsagde sig familiens flercifrede antal præster for at kaste sig over litteraturen.)
171 Rømhild, *Jacob Paludan*. (p. 9: både en standsperson og en unperson i akademiske kredse.)
172 Oldenburg, *Historien om et venskab* (The Story of a Friendship). (p. 18: Brandes' overmand [...] en slagen mand.)
173 Paludan, "Tre Fornavne" (Three First Names). (p. 150: Alle udmærkede Mennesker, men som Kunstnere kun af forbigaaende Interesse for en litterært tidlig antændt Sjæl.)
174 Ibid. (p. 150: Det var som en Færden paa Skyer. Du gode Himmel, dette var jo det levende, alt det jeg syntes jeg kunde mærke i mig selv – det var jo min Verden, Ærkefjenden aabenbarede, det var mod de Aander, jeg droges.)
175 Stengaard, Introduction to *Breve fra Jacob Paludan til Thorvald Petersen* (Letters from Jacob Paludan to Thorvald Petersen). (pp.13–14: absolut et kvalificeret bud på en professor i æstetik).
176 Ibid. (p. 56: der jo aldrig har bestaaet noget egentlig godt Forhold mellem de Gamle og mig. Jeg tror det er noget enestaaende, at en Søn i den Grad lige fra a til z er bundforskellig fra sine Forældre, saa de bogstavelig ikke kan raabe hinanden op, og betragter hinandens Maade at være paa med en rodfæstet Mistænksomhed.)
177 Paludan, "Tre Fornavne" (Three First Names). (p. 150: En færdig Verden, nationalkirkelig-konservativ i datidig Højglans).
178 As reported by: Oldenburg, *Historien om et venskab* (The Story of a Friendship), p. 21.

118   Notes

179 Paludan, *Vink fra en fjern virkelighed* (Signals from a Distant Reality). (p. 90: afguden).
180 Oldenburg, *Historien om et venskab* (The Story of a Friendship). (p. 24: til at ligne berømte familiers sorte får.)
181 Rømhild, *Jacob Paludan*. (p. 12: I en række ungdomsår må det have stået for Stig/Jacob Paludan at hans storebroder var og fik alt det hjemmet ønskede og den akademisk borgerlige tilværelse kunne give).
182 Jacob Paludan, *I høstens månefase* (In the Harvest Phase of the Moon). (p. 76: moseloven krænket). Quoted from: Rømhild, *Jacob Paludan*, p. 18.
183 According to: Stengaard, Introduction to *Breve fra Jacob Paludan til Thorvald Petersen* (Letters from Jacob Paludan to Thorvald Petersen), p. 14.
184 Rømhild, *Jacob Paludan*. (p. 82: Jacob Paludan gifter sig først da storebroderen er død: En forhindring af en slags faldt væk?)
185 Ibid. (p. 11: broderrelationen på godt og ondt har spillet en uhyre rolle for Jacob Paludan – med lange spor i forfatterskabet).
186 Jacob Paludan studied in Copenhagen at *Den Farmaceutiske Læreanstalt*, as the Danish School of Pharmaceutical Sciences, University of Copenhagen, was then known. While a student, Jacob Paludan undertook two pharmacist apprenticeships: in Nykøbing Falster on the island of Falster in south-eastern Denmark, and in Aalborg, North Jutland.
187 Paludan, "Et biografiløst Forfatterliv" (A Biography-less Life as a Writer). (p. 17: Min udeblivende Tilpasning til de overleverede Værdier gjorde det ønskeligt, at jeg kom et andet sted hen, saa mine generende Vurderinger ikke greb ind i Hjemmets daglige Stemning.)
188 From a letter dated 18.12.1918, in: Oldenburg, *Historien om et venskab* (The Story of a Friendship). (p. 108: Hør en prøvet Mands Raad: bliv Vexelfalskner, Voldtægtsforbryder, Meneder, slaa Lygter istykker, drik Radium, stjæl de Fattiges Spareskillinger [...] driv din Kone i Døden og dine Børn paa Sindssygeanstalt – men bliv aldrig Farmaceut.) Henrik Oldenburg quotes from letters written by Jacob Paludan, which he read with permission from the author's widow Vibeke Paludan.
189 The Paludan family moved from a more central part of Copenhagen to the suburb district of Frederiksberg in 1902.
190 Stengaard (ed.), *Breve fra Jacob Paludan til Thorvald Petersen* (Letters

from Jacob Paludan to Thorvald Petersen). (p. 84: kunne leve som jeg ville og arbejde ideelt.) Letter dated 17.6.1929.
191 Ibid. (p. 83: for mig vil det medføre en radikal Livsforandring.) Letter dated 17.6.1929.
192 Ibid. (p. 90: det sundeste, mest tankestyrkende Job der findes). Letter from March 1930.
193 Ibid. (p. 87: Ja, jeg har en Husholderske [...] hun er Gud have Lov helt udenfor den Alder, hvor de falder i Tanker og man selv med, til Gengæld laver hun fornem Mad og holder alting skinnende rent, altsaa et lykkeligt Fund.) Letter dated 24.11.1929.
194 Ibid. (p. 96: Horisont-forandring). Letter dated 25.5.30.
195 At the time of his death, Eberlin owed Jacob Paludan a considerable sum of money.
196 Some of Eric Eberlin's short stories were published in the collection *Americana*, with a foreword written by Jacob Paludan. One of Eberlin's crime stories was included in *På kant med loven – en antologi af danske kriminalhistorier* (Falling Foul of the Law – an anthology of Danish crime stories), Systime, 2003. His two crime novels are: *Døden gaar paa Variete* (1943; Death Goes to the Music Hall) and *Farvel von Falkenow* (1943; Farewell von Falkenow). Poul Houe has written about Eberlin's literary output in "Eric C. Eberlin – en bindestregs-dansker" (Eric C. Eberlin – a hyphenated Dane), *Danske studier* (Danish Studies), vol. 90, C. A. Reitzels Forlag, 1995, and about the play he co-authored with Paludan in "Jacob Paludan og Eric Eberlins sceniske utopi" (The Stage Utopia of Jacob Paludan and Eric Eberlin), *Edda* 94 (Edda. Scandinavian Journal of Literary Research), Universitetsforlaget, 1994.
197 Oldenburg, *Janus fra Thisted. Jacob Paludan som romankunster* (Janus from Thisted. Jacob Paludan as novelist). (p. 226: Som nydelses- og udnyttertype er Otto tegnet meget tæt efter Eric Eberlin). Oldenburg gives a concentrated description (pp. 226–228) of their 'common features' as he sees them. Oldenburg's *Historien om et venskab* (The Story of a Friendship) – about this friendship between Paludan and Eberlin – provides more comprehensive descriptions of Eberlin, which I use in my analysis for further classification of the inspiration to the character of Otto. Flemming Skipper also explores Eberlin and his origins, in the article "Thy i litteraturens vold" (Thy in the Violence of Literature). A short item about Eberlin and his writing can be found in *Dansk skøn-*

litterært forfatterleksikon 1900–1950 (Danish Novelists 1900–1950), vol. 1, Grønholt Pedersens Forlag, 1959.

198 In 1946, Alice Scavenius, née Alice Ninon Duvantier, married Erik Scavenius (1877–1962), Danish foreign minister for several periods and prime minister 1942–1943.

199 Alice Scavenius entrusted the essay to Henrik Oldenburg, who includes a lengthy extract in his book *Historien om et venskab* (The Story of a Friendship). (p. 290: Han havde alle Dyder, og alle elskede ham. Han blev forkælet af alle, og det er farligt [...] han var ikke til at staa for, naar han rullede sin Charmeoffensiv frem.)

200 Obituary quoted in: Oldenburg, *Historien om et venskab* (The Story of a Friendship). (p. 293: Samtidig var han en gudbenaadet Sælger [...] Han manglede heller ikke Stædighed og Vilje til at overtale, hvis det var nødvendigt, og det er mere end en Gang sket, at han har ført en Sag igennem, der for andre dødelige saa haabløs ud [...] Hvor var det overhovedet karakteristisk for ham, at han foretrak den kontante Betaling for den lange Rente. Han var et af de Mennesker, der ikke er skabt til at vente. Han krævede den kontante Udbetaling af Livet.)

201 Foreword: Eberlin, *Americana*. (p. 8 and p. 12: Med sin Charme, sit Vid og sin usædvanlige Højde kaldte [han] paa den Forestilling hos Omverdenen, at han allerede var en hel Mængde – eller i alt fald var et af de Rigdommens Lykkebørn, der kan gøre, hvad der falder dem ind [...] Han var jo alle Overraskelsers og Muligheders Mand, umiddelbart begavet som ingen anden, jeg har kendt. Men han var, om man tør udtrykke sig saaledes, for lang til at ligge i Realiteternes Seng.)

202 Flemming Skipper, "Thy i litteraturens vold" (Thy in the Violence of Literature).

203 Oldenburg, *Janus fra Thisted. Jacob Paludan som romankunster* (Janus from Thisted. Jacob Paludan as novelist). (p. 245: Eric Eberlin har i flere tilfælde leveret stof ('Ideer') til Paludan som kompensation for dennes manglende fantasi).

204 Stengaard (ed.), *Breve fra Jacob Paludan til Thorvald Petersen* (Letters from Jacob Paludan to Thorvald Petersen), p. 86. Letter dated 26.9.1929.

205 Ibid., p. 82, letter dated 30.5.1929.

206 This is apparent from *Breve fra Jacob Paludan til Thorvald Petersen* (Letters from Jacob Paludan to Thorvald Petersen), and from Niels Stengaard's scrupulous comments to the letters. In his

Introduction to the collection, Niels Stengaard also notes that the "Linstow affair" is "given a full orchestration in [...] Otto's fate." (p. 16: Linstow-affæren [...] udsat for fuldt orkester i [...] Ottos skæbne.)

207 *Politiken* 31.5.1929. (p. 15: I Forgaars Aftes udeblev Landsretssagfører Kai Linstow fra sit Hjem, og da han endnu i Gaar Formiddags ikke havde indfundet sig hverken der eller i sin Forretning, gik Familien til Politiet og bad det eftersøge ham. I den senere Tid har Landsretssagføreren lidt af en fremadskridende Sukkersyge, hvis diætetiske Behandling han havde vanskeligt ved at overholde. Det er derfor muligt at han flakker rundt i syg Tilstand. At han skulle have taget sig af Dage, finder de, der er nært knyttet til ham, lidet rimeligt. Lige til det sidste har han været stærkt interesseret i sin Forretning, der er i stærk Blomstring, og hans Familieforhold er de bedst mulige. Vi havde i Aftes en Samtale med Landsretssagførerens Broder, Fuldmægtig Linstow i Statspolitiet, [som sagde:] 'For et halvt Aars Tid siden følte han sig syg, og ved Undersøgelsen viste det sig, at han var angrebet af en alvorlig Sukkersyge. Han tog dog ikke derfor det fornødne Hensyn til sit Helbred . . . Til Tider var han en Del deprimeret, men da min ældste Broder, der er Fuldmægtig hos ham, talte med ham sent i Forgaars Aftes, var der intet usædvanligt at mærke paa ham. Samtalen drejede sig væsentligst om Forretninger. Jeg kan ikke tænke mig andet end, at han flakker syg om.')

208 Stengaard (ed.), *Breve fra Jacob Paludan til Thorvald Petersen* (Letters from Jacob Paludan to Thorvald Petersen). (p. 82: Han har skaffet mig forskellige Værdipapirer, hvis Værdi jeg uundgaaeligt faar Mistanke til [...] Det er dog stadig min bestemte Mening, at Manden er hæderlig, men blot blevet tosset af Overanstrengelse [...].) The letter is dated 30.5.1929, but the article was printed on 31.5.; Jacob Paludan makes clear in the letter that he had broken off writing on 30.5. and resumed the following day, 31.5.

209 *Politiken* 1.6.1929. (p. 15: Den forsvundne Landsretssagfører Linstow [...] menes at være set i Ordrup i Torsdags Aftes. Læderhandler Olsen, der adskillige Gange har set Landsretssagføreren i sit Hjem, sendte Tordags Aften ved 9-Tiden sin 16aarige Søn, der er Piccolo paa Hotel 'Cosmopolite', i Byen efter nogle Kager. Den unge Mand var ledsaget af sin 10aarige Broder. Paa Hyldegaards Tværvej kom en stor lukket

122 *Notes*

Bil imod Drengene i stærk Fart [...] 'Der sidder Landsretssagfører Linstow', sagde Piccoloen til sin Broder, der ogsaa var sikker paa, at det var ham. I Gaar Morges [...] sagde de, hvad de havde set. Naturligvis underrettede Læderhandler Olsen straks Politiet [...] Men herefter taber ethvert Spor sig. Ingen har set noget til Landsretssagføreren, hvis Person er let kendelig. En Formodning om, at han skulde være taget til Göteborg, har ikke bekræftet sig. Af en vis Interesse er det, at man har faaet oplyst, at Hr. Linstow har tilbragt Onsdag Nat paa Palace Hotellet. Efter hans bortgang om Morgenen har Stuepigen fundet Blodpletter, der kunde tyde paa, at han i Nattens Løb har lidt af en Blodstyrtning. En 'Sukkerpatient', der ikke passer sin Kur og faar Blodstyrtning, bliver ofte momentant halvt utilregnelig.)

210 *Politiken* 2.6.1929. (p. 12: Linstow-Mysteriets triste Afslutning. Landsretssagføreren fundet død ved Jægerspris. Landsretssagfører Kai Linstow, som siden i Torsdags Morges har været sporløst forsvundet, er i Gaar fundet død ved Jægerspris. Han havde begaaet Selvmord, idet han havde hængt sig i den 1000aarige Konge-Eg. Ved 4-Tiden cyklede en Arbejdsmand Holger Olsen [...] ud til Konge-Egen, der staar midt i Nordskoven, og her saa han Landsretssagfører Linstows Lig. Olsen underrettede Betjent Petersen i Jægerspris [...] Betjent Petersen [sikrede] sig alle de mange Forretningspapirer, der laa i den Dødes Lommer [...] Mellem Forretningspapirerne fandtes to Breve, et til Afdødes Hustru og et til Broderen, Politifuldmægtig Linstow [...] Efter hvad Undersøgelsen foreløbig viser, har Linstow trods sin Svaghed gaaet den lange Vej derud. I Fredags har han altsaa befundet sig i Frederikssund uden at blive genkendt, til Trods for at Bladene og Radioen har gjort hans Forsvinden kendt vidt og bredt. Han maa altsaa have ført sig med samme Ro som den, der prægede ham under de sidste Samtaler med hans Nærmeste her i Byen. Landsretssagfører Kai Linstow blev kun 33 Aar gammel. Trods sin unge Alder havde han allerede erhvervet sig et Navn som Sagfører, og mange store Sager var efterhaanden blevet ham betroet... I det hele taget var der travl Virksomhed paa Kontoret, Ved Stranden 2, som han delte med Borgmester, Overretssagfører Godskesen. Endelig er Linstows Navn meget kendt i Travkrese, idet han var Ejer af en Stald paa 4 Heste. Han var en munter, livsglad Mand, der samlede sig Venner, hvor han viste sig. Han efterlader sig Hustru og to Børn.)

211 Stengaard (ed.), *Breve fra Jacob Paludan til Thorvald Petersen* (Letters from Jacob Paludan to Thorvald Petersen). (p. 82 and p. 84: Ja, det var – det var en grusom Salve, og jeg er ikke kommet til Hægterne endnu. Min gamle 'Ven', Skolekammerat etc. etc. gik ud og hængte sig i Kongeegen, efter som min betroede i financielle Sager at have holdt Hus for mine Penge (og andres) i 5 Aar, snydt og bedraget paa enhver tænkelig Maade og derefter overladende mig, sin Familie og mange andre til at lede i Ruinerne [...] dog ærgrer jeg mig ikke ved at gaa og regne ud, hvad jeg kunde have købt for de Penge, Fyren har holdt Travstald for.) Letter dated 17.6.1929.
212 *Politiken* 4.6.1929. (p. 12: I øvrigt er der ikke til Politiet indløbet nogen Anmodning fra Privatpersoner om en Undersøgelse.)
213 *Politiken* 3.6.1929. (p. 5: Ved Middagstid har han indfundet sig i Forpagtergarden i Dyrnæs, hvor Fru Carlsen paa hans Anmodning har serveret en Kop Kaffe for ham. Hun har forklaret, at han gjorde et meget nervøst Indtryk. Sveden dryppede fra hans Pande, og han snakkede ustandseligt. Blandt andet sagde han, at han var godt kendt paa Egnen, hvor han havde færdedes meget som Barn. Han var nu ude for at genopfriske de gamle Indtryk. Da han gik, lagde hun Mærke til, at han vaklede.)
214 Stengaard (ed.), *Breve fra Jacob Paludan til Thorvald Petersen* (Letters from Jacob Paludan to Thorvald Petersen). (p. 83: Han havde ved denne Termin Valget mellem Forbedringshuset ("Køleren") eller – det andet, og han valgte, ikke uden Klogskab, den grufulde Udvej.) Letter dated 17.6.1929. In note 214, Niels Stengaard writes: "the house of correction was introduced as a type of prison in 1789 and closed down in 1933." (p. 123: Forbedringshuset oprettedes som Fængselstype 1789 og blev nedlagt 1933.)
215 Ibid. (p. 83: Naturligvis har jeg forsømt mig grovelig ved ikke at føre strengere Kontrol [...] min Tillid til Mennesker maa sagtelig repareres.) Letter dated 17.6.1929.
216 Oldenburg, *Historien om et venskab* (The Story of a Friendship). (p. 250: Når Paludan fra tid til anden havde spurgt til sin formue, fik han at vide, at den var anbragt i fast ejendom, og som bevis blev han fragtet med ud på Nørrebro og fik forevist et par store boligblokke. Senere skulle det vise sig, at Paludans penge aldrig nåede så langt.) In note 70, p. 333, Henrik Oldenburg states that

124 Notes

he heard this from Paludan-scholar Børge Benthien, who had in turn been told the story by Jacob Paludan himself.
217 Stengaard (ed.), *Breve fra Jacob Paludan til Thorvald Petersen* (Letters from Jacob Paludan to Thorvald Petersen). (p. 85: intet jo er saa galt, uden at det er godt for noget). Letter dated 26.9.1929.
218 Frandsen, *Aargangen der maatte snuble i Starten* (The Generation that Could Not Help Stumbling at the Start). (p. 9: Jacob Paludan er den mest læste af 1920'ernes Forfattere. Jeg har en Januardag 1942 gennemtrawlet Københavns Antikvariater uden at opdrive et eneste af hans Værker. Overalt gav man det samme Svar, at en Bog af Paludan gaar samme Dag, den kommer. Bibliotekernes Udlaansprotokoller fortæller noget lignende.)
219 *Jørgen Stein*, 2014. (p. 7: Min generation fik *Jørgen Stein* i konfirmationsgave, og jeg blev fanget ind, slugte Paludans andre bøger og citerede ham i mine stile. Den blev kaldt 'gymnasiasternes bibel', og det *var* den, læst i laser af os 15–18-årige. I undersøgelser kom Paludan ud som gymnasiasternes yndlingsforfatter – foran Steinbeck, Hemingway og Remarque. Det skyldtes, skrev jeg i en meget 17-årig hyldest på hans 60-årsdag i 1956, at *Jørgen Stein* så ægte beskrev vores alders "vanskeligheder, følelser og fornemmelser".)
220 Danish author Leif Panduro (1923–1977) and his colleague Klaus Rifbjerg were the literary standard-bearers in the showdown with 1950s morality, and they thereby blazed a trail for the youth rebellion of the 1960s, in which they also took an active part.
221 *Jørgen Stein*, 2014. (p. 8: modernismen og 70'ernes ideologikritik skar hans [Paludans] romaner ned).
222 Zerlang, "På sporet af Paludan" (Tracking Paludan), *Bogens Verden*, no. 5, 1989. (p. 378: Nej, hvis navnet Paludan er ved at forsvinde fra den større læserverdens landkort, skyldes det snarere, at den "ynglingepsykologi" (Rømhild), som afgrænser forfatterskabets territorium, ikke er et landskab, moderne ynglingesjæle finder sig hjemme i. Jørgen Stein med alle hans kvalfulde frustrationer gjorde ham til et spejlbillede for den ældre gymnasieungdom, men for gymnasieungdommen har frustrationer siden 60ernes slutning mest været et felt for teknik og tidsbegrænset lidelse.) In the parenthesis, Zerlang is referring to: Rømhild, *Jacob Paludan*.
223 Hertel, "Litteraturens børsnoteringer" (Literary Stock Exchange), *Politiken* 16.11.2014. Hans Hertel describes his very

positive surprise when re-reading *Jørgen Stein* for the Foreword to the 2014 republication. He adds: "In the re-reading, I have also found gold in Paludan's early books, and especially in his essay writing." (Ved genlæsning har jeg også fundet guld i Paludans første bøger og især i hans essaykunst.) The article is included in Hans Hertel's book *Bogmennesker. Bøger og bogfolk – essays og portrætter 1991–2016* (Book People. Books and the Book Community – Essays and Portraits 1991–2016).
224 16.2.2015. (Kan unge læsere i dag leve med i, eller bare begribe den unge Jørgen Steins verden [...] kan Jørgen Steins liv og skæbne være spejl for en ung i det 21. århundrede? / Der er faktisk også lidt moderne tv-serie over skildringen af Ottos skæbne (Jørgens bror).)
225 Oldenburg, *Historien om et venskab* (The Story of a Friendship), pp. 272–275.
226 In his review "Jacob Paludans nye Bog" (Jacob Paludan's New Book), *Dagens Nyheder* 7.9.1933. (en lille fortræffelig Roman i Romanen / Saadan skal en Bog skrives).
227 In his review "Jacob Paludans Roman" (Jacob Paludan's Novel), *Politiken* 6.9.1933. (De to bærer Romanens Spænding, for Romantekniker det er Jacob Paludan). Elsewhere in the review, Tom Kristensen writes: "Jacob Paludan is our youngest classical author [...] Furthermore, he is just as good an artist as Henrik Pontoppidan" (Jacob Paludan er vor yngste, klassiske forfatter [...] Desuden er han lige saa god en Kunstner som Henrik Pontoppidan) – and Henrik Pontoppidan was the 1917 Nobel laureate in literature!
228 In the journal *Tilskueren* (The Spectator), November 1933. (p. 347: overbeviser hele Vejen, og dens tragiske Endeligt er givet med stor Styrke).
229 Møller Kristensen, *Dansk litteratur 1918–1950* (Danish Literature 1918–1950). (p. 70: Det er en levende og dramatisk illustration til efterkrigstidens historie. Otto er en ligesaa anskuelig figur, som Jørgen er sløret og uhåndgribelig. / Som et modstykke til den idealistisk søgende Jørgen staar den ældre broder Otto, der gaar i stykker på den rene materialisme. Han er nydelsesmenneske af karakter.)
230 Nielsen, "Den store spiller" (The Big Player), essay in *Politiken* newspaper, 27.7.1992. (Romanen om generationen der snublede i starten, er romanen blevet kaldt, men den fremstår dog i dag

først og fremmest som et spejl af en tid, der sjovt nok på visse områder kan minde ganske godt om de 80'ere, vi lige har lagt bag os med fænomener som fejlslagne spekulationer i erhvervslivet, pengefetichisme og fravær af sammenhæng mellem penge og moral.) The phrase "generation that could not help stumbling at the start" (generationen der snublede i starten) refers to the final sentence in *Jørgen Stein* and to the title of Ernst Frandsen's renowned book: *Aargangen der maatte snuble i Starten* (The Generation that Could Not Help Stumbling at the Start).
231 Ibid. (den gamle historie om Otto Stein). Preben Erik Nielsen refers to three individuals: *Johannes Petersen* (1925–1990) was CEO and later chairman of the board of directors for the Danish textile company Nordisk Fjer, which grew into an international business group. He had been committing fraud against the company for many years; when this was uncovered, he committed suicide. *Klaus Riskær Pedersen* is a Danish businessman with several convictions for fraud and embezzlement, resulting in prison sentences. *Per Villum Hansen* was CEO of Hafnia, a major Danish insurance company, but was dismissed in 1992, charged with illegal share investment; the case went to court, he was acquitted.
232 Ibid. (I skrivende stund toner tre aktuelle skikkelser frem, der hver på sin måde dækker de mentale træk og adfærden, der i indeværende sammenhæng er blevet benævnt erhvervslivets 'gamblere', nemlig Johannes Petersen fra Nordisk Fjer, Klaus Riskær Pedersen og Per Villum Hansen fra Hafnia [...] De skulle ud og gå på vandet, før de blev afsløret som falske profeter [...] Bestyrelserne har været optaget af andre forhold og har åbenbart ikke været inde i væsentlige sider af den daglige drift. Den administrerende direktør har ledet selskabet, som om det var hans eget, og glemt, at det var et ansvar, der var til låns. Store mislykkede investeringer er blevet mødt med nye storinvesteringer, som der sjældent har været kapitalmæssig dækning for ud fra et sikkerhedsprincip. Der er blevet lukket 'huller' i én uendelighed. Der er blevet afleveret uigennemsigtige og mangelfulde regnskaber [...] Og da tæppet endelig gik, stod det pludselig klart for alle, at situationen var langt værre end de værste forestillinger.)
233 Ibid. (Selv i den bedste familie kan der forekomme 'sorte får').
234 Ibid. (et moderne menneske / Hver tid producerer sin Otto Stein og sine 'gamblere'.)

235 Schou, "Provins og apokalypse. Jacob Paludan: *Jørgen Stein*" (Province and Apocalypse. Jacob Paludan: *Jørgen Stein*). (p. 232: Beretningen om Ottos stadig mere desperate forretnings- og forhalingsaffærer og hans sluttelige selvmord er endnu grusom læsning. Med sin fint justerede balance mellem tragik og satire er den et mere magtfuldt udtryk for romanens kritik af den moderne civilisation end Jørgens retræte til Havnstrup [...] Det musikalsk-stilistiske mesterskab, han udfolder i skildringen af tyver-yuppiernes amokløb efter guldet for enden af regnbuen, vil sikre *Jørgen Stein*s klassiker-status. Længe efter at romanens positive modbillede har tabt sin stråleglans.)

BIBLIOGRAPHY

All published translated titles are in italic typeface; unpublished translated titles are in normal typeface.

This bibliography includes all the books and articles about Jacob Paludan to which I have referred while writing *Portrait of a Danish Conman*; these works are entered in the section: "Most relevant literature about Jacob Paludan and Otto Stein". I have also included the works on Jacob Paludan that are not of direct relevance to the study of Otto Stein; the titles of these works have not been translated into English, but are entered in the section: "Further reading about Jacob Paludan (Danish)".

Works by Jacob Paludan
Novels

Various editions of Jacob Paludan's novels are available; I have chosen those listed. Two of the novels, *Fugle omkring Fyret* and *Jørgen Stein*, have been published in English translation.

De vestlige Veje (1922; The Western Roads), Hans Reitzel, 1962.
Søgelys (1923; Searchlight), Hans Reitzel, 1960.
En Vinter lang (1924; Winter Long), Steen Hasselbalchs Forlag, 1924.
Fugle omkring Fyret (1925), Steen Hasselbalchs Forlag, 1927. *Birds Around the Light*, translated from the Danish by Grace Isabel Colbron, G. P. Putnam's Sons, 1928.
Markerne modnes (1927; The Fields are Ripening), Steen Hasselbalchs Forlag, 1962.
Jørgen Stein (1933), Steen Hasselbalchs Forlag, 1948. Translated from the Danish by Carl Malmberg, University of Wisconsin Press, 1966.

Essays

The following are the essays written by Jacob Paludan used in this book; he wrote innumerable other essays.

"I det skraa, øjenblændende Sollys" (In the Oblique, Dazzling Sunlight). In *Han gik Ture* (He Went for Walks), essays, Gyldendal, 1949.
"Ved Overtagelsen af en jysk Hytte" (On Taking Over a Cabin in Jutland). In *Han gik Ture* (He Went for Walks), essays, Gyldendal, 1949.
"Den unge Dostojefski" (The Young Dostoevsky). In *Litterært Selskab* (Literary Society), essays, Steen Hasselbalchs Forlag, 1956.
"Notater om Thomas Mann" (Notes on Thomas Mann). In *Litterært Selskab* (Literary Society), essays, Steen Hasselbalchs Forlag, 1956.
"Et biografiløst Forfatterliv" (A Biography-less Life as a Writer). In *Siden De Spørger – og andre Omkredsninger* (Since You Ask – and Other Encirclements), essays, Steen Hasselbalchs Forlag, 1968.
"Tre Fornavne" (Three First Names). In *Siden De Spørger – og andre Omkredsninger* (Since You Ask – and Other Encirclements), essays, Steen Hasselbalchs Forlag, 1968.
I høstens månefase (In the Harvest Phase of the Moon), essays, Gyldendal, 1973.
Vink fra en fjern virkelighed (Signals from a Distant Reality), essays, Gyldendal, 1975.

Other writings

Niels Stengaard (ed.), *Breve fra Jacob Paludan til Thorvald Petersen* (Letters from Jacob Paludan to Thorvald Petersen), Museum Tusculanums Forlag, 1999.
Foreword to: Eric Eberlin, *Americana*, Carit Andersens Forlag, 1944.

Most relevant literature about Jacob Paludan and Otto Stein

Barfoed, Niels. "*Jørgen Stein* und Thomas Mann". In *Nerthus: Nordischdeutsche Beiträge*, Vol. III, Eugen Diederichs Verlag, 1972.
Barfoed, Niels. "Pietetens helvede. Jacob Paludans *Jørgen Stein*" (The Hell that is Respect, Jacob Paludan's *Jørgen Stein*). In *Tilbageblik på 30'erne. Litteratur, teater, kulturdebat 1930–39*. En antologi ved Hans Hertel (Looking Back at the 1930s. Literature, theatre, cultural debate 1930-39. An anthology edited by Hans Hertel), Aschehoug, 1997.
Benthien, Børge. *Jacob Paludan / En bibliografi* (Jacob Paludan / A Bibliography), Gyldendal, 1980.
Bondebjerg, Ib. "Borgerlig individualisme i havsnød" (Bourgeois

130 Bibliography

Individualism in Distress). In *Dansk litteraturhistorie* 7 (History of Danish Literature, vol. 7), Gyldendal, 1984.

Brix, Hans. "Jacob Paludans nye Bog" (Jacob Paludan's New Book). Review in *Dagens Nyheder* newspaper, 7.9.1933.

la Cour, Paul. Review of *Jørgen Stein*. In *Tilskueren* journal (The Spectator), Gyldendal, November 1933.

Dansk skønlitterært forfatterleksikon 1900–1950 (Danish Novelists 1900-1950), vol. 1, Grønholt Pedersens Forlag, 1959.

Frandsen, Ernst. *Aargangen der maatte snuble i Starten* (The Generation that Could Not Help Stumbling at the Start), Gyldendal, 1943.

Frederiksen, Emil. *Jacob Paludan*, Gyldendal, 1966.

Hansen, Per Krogh. "Jacob Paludan". In *Danske digtere i det 20. århundrede* (Twentieth-Century Danish Writers), vol. 1, ed. Anne-Marie Mai, Gads Forlag, 2002.

Hertel, Hans. *Bogmennesker. Bøger og bogfolk – essays og portrætter 1991–2016* (Book People. Books and the Book Community – Essays and Portraits 1991-2016), Tiderne Skifter, 2016.

Hertel, Hans. Foreword to: Jacob Paludan. *Jørgen Stein*, Gyldendal, 2014.

Hertel, Hans. "Litteraturens børsnoteringer" (Literary Stock Exchange), *Politiken* newspaper, 16.11.2014.

Houe, Poul. "Eric C. Eberlin – en bindestregs-dansker" (Eric C. Eberlin – a hyphenated Dane). In *Danske studier* (Danish Studies), vol. 90, C. A. Reitzels Forlag, 1995.

Houe, Poul. *Fra Amerika til Danmark. På rejse gennem Jacob Paludans ungdomsromaner* (From America to Denmark. A journey through Jacob Paludan's early novels), Museum Tusculanums Forlag, 1993.

Houe, Poul. "Jacob Paludan og Eric Eberlins sceniske utopi" (The Stage Utopia of Jacob Paludan and Eric Eberlin). In *Edda* 94 (Edda. Scandinavian Journal of Literary Research), Universitetsforlaget, 1994.

Høst, Beth. "'Jørgen Stein' af Jacob Paludan" ('Jørgen Stein' by Jacob Paludan), www.litteratursiden.dk/anmeldelser.

Kehler, Henning. *Paa Jagt efter Geniet* (Pursuing the Genius), Nyt Nordisk Forlag, Arnold Busck, 1938.

Kristensen, Sven Møller. *Dansk litteratur 1918–1950* (Danish Literature 1918-1950), Munksgaard, 1950.

Kristensen, Tom. "Jacob Paludans Roman" (Jacob Paludan's Novel). Review in *Politiken* newspaper, 6.9.1933.

Lundbo, Orla. *Jacob Paludan*, Steen Hasselbalchs Forlag, 1943.

Bibliography 131

Mai, Anne-Marie and Dalager, Stig. *Litteraturteori og analysestrategi* (Literary Theory and Analytic Strategy), Arkona, 1978.

Nielsen, Preben Erik. "Den store spiller" (The Big Player), article in *Politiken* newspaper, 27.7.1992.

Oldenburg, Henrik. *Historien om et venskab* (The Story of a Friendship), Gyldendal, 1984.

Oldenburg, Henrik. *Janus fra Thisted. Jacob Paludan som romankunster* (Janus from Thisted. Jacob Paludan as novelist), Gyldendal, 1988.

Politiken newspaper, 31.5.1929.

Politiken newspaper, 1.6.1929.

Politiken newspaper, 2.6.1929.

Politiken newspaper, 3.6.1929.

Politiken newspaper, 4.6.1929.

Rømhild, Lars Peter. *Jacob Paludan*, AIL 112 (working papers from Institut for Litteraturvidenskab/Department of Comparative Literature, University of Copenhagen), 1980.

Rømhild, Lars Peter. "Jacob Paludan". In *Danske digtere i det 20. århundrede* (Twentieth-Century Danish Writers), vol. 2, eds. Mette Winge and Torben Brostrøm, Gads Forlag, 1981.

Schou, Søren. "Provins og apokalypse. Jacob Paludan: *Jørgen Stein*" (Province and Apocalypse. Jacob Paludan: *Jørgen Stein*). In *Læsninger i dansk litteratur* (Studies in Danish Literature), vol. 3, Odense Universitetsforlag, 1997.

Skipper, Flemming. www.thistedmuseum.dk/paludan. www. arkiv.thisted-bibliotek.dk/Paludan.

Skou-Hansen, Tage. "Forsvar for prosaen" (In Defence of Prose). In *Heretica. En antologi* (Heretica. An anthology), ed. Ole Wivel, Gyldendal, 1962 / 1976.

Stengaard, Niels. Introduction to: *Breve fra Jacob Paludan til Thorvald Petersen* (Letters from Jacob Paludan to Thorvald Petersen), Museum Tusculanums Forlag, 1999.

Sørensen, Marianne. "Jørgen Stein". In *Kritik 93*, Gyldendal, 1990.

Zerlang, Martin. "På sporet af Paludan" (Tracking Paludan). In *Bogens Verden*, no. 5, 1989.

Zerlang, Martin and Reinvaldt, Henrik. "Man kan ikke male ud over rammen. Om klassebevidsthed og karakterstruktur i Jacob Paludans *Jørgen Stein*" (You Cannot Paint Beyond the Frame. On class consciousness and character structure in Jacob Paludan's *Jørgen Stein*). In *Analyser af danske romaner 3* (Analyses of Danish Novels 3), Borgens Forlag, 1977.

Zerlang, Martin. Review of the Danish edition of *Portrait of a Danish Conman* by Frantz Leander Hansen. In "Scandinavian Studies", Vol. 92, No. 2, 2020, University of Illinois Press.

Secondary Sources

Andersen, Hans Christian. "The Shadow" (1847).
Bakhtin, Mikhail. *Problems of Dostoevsky's Poetics* (1929 / 1963), edited and translated from the Russian by Caryl Emerson, *Theory and History of Literature*, vol. 8, University of Minnesota Press, 1984.
Bang, Herman. *Håbløse slægter* (1880) (Hopeless Generations), Carit Andersens Forlag, 1966.
Bang, Herman. *Stuk* (1887) (Stucco), Gyldendal, 2004.
Blixen, Karen. "The Deluge at Norderney". In *Seven Gothic Tales* (1934), Penguin Books, 1963.
Dostoevsky, Anna. *Dostoevsky: Reminiscences*, Liveright Paperback, 1975 / 1977.
Dostoevsky, Fyodor. *The Brothers Karamazov* (1880), iBoo Press, 2020.
Dostoevsky, Fyodor. *Crime and Punishment* (1866), translated from the Russian by Nicolas Pasternak Slater, Oxford University Press, 2017.
Dostoevsky, Fyodor. *The Gambler* (1866), iBoo Press, 2020.
Fitzgerald, F. Scott. *The Great Gatsby* (1926), Penguin, 1978.
Frandsen, Finn. "Begæret, volden og offeret" (The Desire, the Violence and the Victim). In *Religionsvidenskabeligt Tidsskrift* 6 (Journal of Religious Studies no. 6), University of Aarhus, 1985.
Girard, René. *Deceit, Desire & the Novel*, John Hopkins University Press, 1965 / 1976.
Girard, René. *Violence and the Sacred*, Bloomsbury Academic, 1988 / 2013.
Hansen, Frantz Leander. "Djævleblændt teologi. Livskraft og tilgivelse i Dostojevskijs 'store' romaner" (Consummate theology. Vitality and forgiveness in Dostoevsky's 'major' novels). In *Bogens Verden* (The World of Books), no. 3, Dansk Biblioteksforening og Studiekredsforeningen, 2005.
Hansen, Martin A. *Løgneren*, Gyldendal, 1950.
Hansen, Martin A. *The Liar* (1950) (*Løgneren*), translated from the Danish by John Jeppson Egglishaw, Los Angeles, Sun & Moon Press, 1995.
Jensen, Hans J. Lundager. *René Girard*, Anis, 1991.
Joyce, James. *Ulysses* (1922), Penguin Books, 1984, in association with The Bodley Head, 1960.

Kristensen, Tom: *Hærværk* (1930), Gyldendal, 1972.
Kristensen, Tom: *Havoc* (1930) (*Hærværk*), translated from the Danish by Carl Malmberg, University of Wisconsin Press, 1968. Reprinted by New York Review Books Classics, 2018, with an introduction by Morten Høi Jensen.
Larsen, Henrik. *Alberti-Katastrofen* (The Alberti Disaster), Forlaget Politisk Revy, 1996.
Lawrence, D. H. *Lady Chatterley's Lover* (1928).
Mann, Thomas. *Bekenntnisse des Hochstaplers Felix Krull. Der Memoiren, erster Teil*, S. Fischer Verlag, 1954. (*The Confessions of Felix Krull, Confidence Man: The Early Years*).
Mann, Thomas. *Buddenbrooks – Verfall einer Familie*, S. Fischer Verlag, 1901.
Mann, Thomas. *Buddenbrooks: The Decline of a Family*, translated from the German by John E. Woods, Everyman's Library, 1994.
Panduro, Leif. *Rend mig i traditionerne*, Gyldendal, 1958.
Panduro, Leif. *Kick Me in the Traditions* (*Rend mig i traditionerne*), translated from the Danish by Carl Malmberg, Eriksson-Taplinger Company, 1961.
Remarque, Erich Maria. *All Quiet on the Western Front* (1929).
Rifbjerg, Klaus. *Den kroniske uskyld,* Gyldendal, 1958.
Rifbjerg, Klaus. *Terminal Innocence* (*Den kroniske uskyld*), translated from the Danish by Paul Larkin, Norvik Press, 2015.
Rifbjerg, Klaus. *Nøleren* (The Delayer), Gyldendal, 2012.
Sartre, Jean-Paul. *Qu'est-ce que la littérature?* Librairie Gallimard, 1948.
Sartre, Jean-Paul. *What is Literature?* (*Qu'est-ce que la littérature?*) Translated from the French by Bernard Frechtman (1950), Methuen: Routledge Classics, 2001.

Further reading about Jacob Paludan (Danish)

Bager, Poul. *Læsninger. Analyser af udvalgte tekster*, Centrum, 1991.
Bodelsen, Anders. Efterskrift til *Jørgen Stein,* Gyldendals Bibliotek, 1964.
Brask, Peter. "Den diskrete charmetrold. Kritiske betragtninger over et Paludan-citat". In *danske studier 1987,* C. A. Reitzels Forlag.
Brostrøm, Torben. "Jacob Paludan på Sporet af den tabte Tid". In *Dansk Litteratur Historie*, vol. 4, ed. P. H. Traustedt, Politikens Forlag, 1966.
Dansk Biografisk Leksikon. "Jacob Paludan", www.denstoredanske.dk.
Eberlin, Eric. *Americana,* Carit Andersens Forlag, 1944.

134 Bibliography

Eberlin, Eric. Crime novels: *Døden gaar paa Variete* (1943) and *Farvel von Falkenow* (1943). One of his crime stories is published in: *På kant med loven – en antologi af danske kriminalhistorier*, Systime, 2003.

Elfelt, Kjeld. *Skribenter i Skriftestolen*, Privattryk, 1944.

Franzén, Lars-Olof. "Skuddene i Sarajevo 1932". In *Punktnedslag i dansk litteratur 1880-1970*, Lindhardt og Ringhof, 1971.

Frederiksen, Emil. "Jacob Paludan". In *Danske digtere i det 20. århundrede*, vol. 2, eds. Frederik Nielsen and Ole Restrup, Gads Forlag, 1966.

Hallar, Søren. *Jacob Paludan*, Steen Hasselbalchs Forlag, 1928.

Handesten, Lars. *Litterære rejser – poetik og erkendelse i danske digteres rejsebøger*, C. A. Reitzels Forlag, 1992.

Hansen, Thorkild. *De søde piger. Dagbog 1943-47*, Gyldendal, 1974.

Hansen, Thorkild. *Minder svøbt i vejr. En studie i Jacob Paludans romaner*, Steen Hasselbalchs Forlag, 1947.

Houe, Poul. "Dråbespil og dråbespild. I anledning af Jacob Paludans 100 års dag". In *Bogens Verden* no. 1, 1996.

Jensen, Kamilla. "Dannelsesroman eller udviklingsroman: En genrediskussion ud fra *Lykke-Per* og *Jørgen Stein*". In *Synsvinkler*. Årg. 17, no. 37, 2008.

Jensen, S. Haugstrup. "Jacob Paludan". In *Kapitler af dansk digtning fra Herman Bang til Kaj Munk*, Det Danske Forlag, 1951.

Jessen, Jørn. *Die Zeitkritik in den Romanen Jacob Paludans*. Doktorafhandling 1974, Christian-Albrechts-Universität zu Kiel.

Jørgensen, Jens Anker and Wentzel, Knud. *Hovedsporet. Dansk litteraturs historie*, Gyldendal, 2005.

Kehler, Henning. "Jacob Paludans store Roman". Review of *Jørgen Stein* i *Berlingske Tidende*, 6.9.1933.

Kjølbye, Marie Louise. "Matmanden – at genlæse Jørgen Stein". In *Tekster vi hader*, ed. Johan Rosdahl, Dansklærerforeningen, 2001.

Kofoed, Niels V. *Jacob Paludan – ambivalensens digter*, ABC Publishing, 2016.

Kondrup, Johnny. *Erindringens udveje. Studier i moderne dansk selvbiografi*, Amadeus, 1994.

Laigaard, Jens. "Paludan og musikken", www.musikbiblioteket.dk, 2006.

Larsen, Ole Kjær. *Den private fortid og samtiden, en belysning af tidsproblematikken i Jacob Paludans romaner*, dissertation 1972, University of Copenhagen.

Bibliography 135

Levy, Jette Lundbo. "Krig og krisetider". In *Litteraturhistorier. Perspektiver på dansk teksthistorie 1700-1970*, DR, 1994.
Lundbo, Orla. *Hilsen til Jacob Paludan paa Halvtredsaarsdagen*, Steen Hasselbalchs Forlag, 1946.
Lundbo, Orla. "Jacob Paludan". In *Danmarks store digtere. Dansk Litteratur-Haandbog*, ed. Hakon Stangerup, Skandinavisk Bogforlag, 1944.
Madsen, Peter. "Kontinuitetens abstrakte overvindelse, om Jacob Paludan: *Fugle omkring Fyret*". In *Tekstanalyser, ideologikritiske tekster*, Munksgaard, 1973.
Musarra-Schrøder, Ulla. "Modernismen i 30'ernes danske litteratur (Tom Kristensen, Jacob Paludan, Hans Kirk)". In *Mellemkrigstid. Litterære og sproglige essays*, 1981, Tijdschrift voor Skandinavistiek.
Normann, Marie. "Hvorfor blev Jacob Paludan essayist?". In *Danske studier 1990*, C. A. Reitzels Forlag.
Nørgaard, Felix. "Jacob Paludan". In *Danske Digtere i det 20. Aarhundrede. Fra Johannes V. Jensen til den unge Lyrik*, eds. Ernst Frandsen and Niels Kaas Johansen, vol. 1. Gads Forlag, 1951.
Overø, Jens. *Jacob Paludan – forfatter, farmaceut og Birkerødborger*, Birkerød Apotek, 1998.
Pahuus, Mogens. "Jacob Paludan: 'Jørgen Stein'". In *Uendelighedslængsel*, Forlaget Philosophia, 1998.
Reinvaldt, Henrik. *Den tidligborgerlige dannelse i krise. En socialhistorisk analyse af Jacob Paludans romaner*, dissertation 1976, University of Copenhagen.
Rømhild, Lars Peter. *Jyllands-Posten*s kronik, 7.2.1996.
Rømhild, Lars Peter. "Paludans erindring. I anledning af Jacob Paludans 100 års dag". In *Bogens Verden* no. 1, 1996.
Schou, Søren. "Blasert barberi – da danske forfattere mødte jazzen". In *Spring* no. 6, 1994.
Schou, Søren. "Slægten som Pejlemærke – Jacob Paludan". In *Dansk litteraturs historie 1920-1960*, vol. 4, eds. May Schack and Klaus P. Mortensen, Gyldendal, 2006.
Skov, Mia Egander. "At finde vej". In *Replique*, 2012.
Skøt, Ib. "Lykke-Per og Jørgen Stein". In *Bogens Verden* no. 2, 1990.
Stangerup, Hakon. *Den unge litteratur. Essais*, Steen Hasselbalchs Forlag, 1928.
Stangerup, Hakon. Introduction to *Jacob Paludan. Et udvalg ved Hakon Stangerup*, Dansklærerforeningen, Gyldendal, 1960.

Bibliography

Stengaard, Niels. *Nutidens og fortidens terræn. En studie i tidsopfattelsen i Jacob Paludans essays,* dissertation 1971, University of Copenhagen.

Svendsen, Erik. "Myren i metropolen. Jacob Paludans *Jørgen Stein*". In *Københavner Romaner,* eds. Marianne Barlyng and Søren Schou, Borgen, 1996.

Sørensen, Lise. "Jørgen Steins damer". In *Digternes damer,* Gyldendal, 1964.

Vesterdal, Annemarie. *Opfattelsen af kunsten og kunstneren i Jacob Paludans univers,* dissertation 1966, University of Copenhagen.

Woel, Cai M. *Tyvernes og Tredvernes Digtere,* vol. 2, Asa's Forlag, 1941.

INDEX

Aargangen der maatte snuble i Starten (The Generation that Could Not Help Stumbling at the Start) (Frandsen), 97
Alberti, Peter Adler, 42–43, 43, 51, 110n95, 110n96
Alberti-Katastrofen (The Alberti Disaster) (Larsen), 43
All Quiet on the Western Front (Remarque), 61
Americana (Eberlin), 87, 119n196
Andersen, Hans Christian, 29
Andersen, Hartvig, 87
Austro-Hungarian Empire, The, 3

Bakhtin, Mikhail, 105n36
Bagger, Stein, 101
Bang, Herman, 4–5, 34–35, 101
Barfoed, Niels, 11, 56, 104–105n26
Benthien, Børge, 123–124n216
Birds Around the Light (*Fugle omkring Fyret*) (Paludan), ix, 42, 67–69, 81
and Paludan's other novels, ix, 76–77, 112n119
Blixen, Karen, 37
Bondebjerg, Ib, 33
Brandes, Georg, 79, 80
Brix, Hans, 99
Brothers Karamazov, The (Dostoevsky), 42
Buddenbrooks (Mann), 5–6, 9–11, 27, 34, 51–52, 104–105n26

la Cour, Poul, 57, 99
Crime and Punishment (Dostoevsky), 30, 40, 41, 60, 111n100

Dalager, Stig, 52, 111n104
De vestlige Veje (The Western Roads) (Paludan), 59–61, 116–117n165
and *Markerne modnes* (The Fields are Ripening), 74–75
and Paludan's other novels, ix, 76–77, 112n119
Deceit, Desire & the Novel (Girard), 111n101
"Deluge at Norderney, The" (Blixen), 37
desire
 mimetic and triangular, 49–51
Dostoevsky, Anna, 27–28
Dostoevsky, Fyodor, 14–15, 27–28, 30, 40, 41, 42, 45, 51, 105n36, 111n100

Eberlin, Eric, 84, 85–88, 95, 119n195, 119n196
Ecuador, xiv, 59, 63, 82, 85
En Vinter lang (Winter Long) (Paludan), 64–67, 69
and *The Liar* (Hansen), 65–67
and Paludan's other novels, ix, 76–77, 112n119
Essay
 Paludan as essay writer, xiv, 54, 77, 124–125n223

Europe, 3
father and son theme, 4, 8–9, 10, 17–18, 19–20, 43, 49, 51, 72–73, 80–81
Felix Krull, The Confessions of (Mann), 11
Ferdinand, Frans, 3
First World War, The, 3, 7, 20, 49, 51, 57, 59, 66, 67, 70, 76
Fitzgerald, Francis Scott, 9
Frandsen, Ernst, 57, 97, 114–115n146
fraud, 11, 62, 67–69, 88–95
  as a consequence of ambition, 8–9, 16, 21, 51, 60, 82–83
  the conman's makeup, vii, 20, 24, 47
  and culture / society, vii, 9–11, 23, 26, 34–35, 39, 41–42, 42–43, 49–51, 52, 76–77, 99–102
  as an existential condition, vii, 20, 26–27, 49–51, 76
  due to pressure of expectation, 12–13, 19, 46, 82
  and family relationships, 6–7, 9–11, 43
  as fantasist, 17, 18–19, 20, 46–47, 51
  and the life of fashionable society, 9, 18–21, 22–23, 68, 76
  and lack of sense of guilt, 22, 23–24, 34, 41, 47
  and love, 20, 72, 76
  rather than poverty, 17–18, 47, 48–49
  and rivalry, 49–51
  summing up, 46–49
  topicality, vii, 97–102
  and sense of invulnerability, 6, 46
  as phenomenon in the 1920s,

vii, 22, 27, 46–49, 49–51, 61, 65, 76–77, 101
Fraud Squad, The, vii
Frederik VII, King, 5
Frederiksen, Emil, 14, 23

Gambler, The (Dostoevsky), 27–28
Girard, René, 49–51, 111n101
Goethe, Johann Wolfgang, 15
Goos, August Herman Ferdinand Carl, 110n96
Great Britain, 57
Great Gatsby, The (Scott Fitzgerald), 9, 22

Hafnia, 100, 126n231
Hamsun, Knut, 114–115n146
Hansen, Martin A., 65–66
Hansen, Per Villum, 100, 126n231
Havoc (*Hærværk*) (Kristensen) and *Søgelys* (Searchlight), 64
Hemingway, Ernest, 97
Hertel, Hans, viii, 97–98, 124–125n223
Houe, Poul, 119n196
Høst, Beth, 98–99
Håbløse slægter (Hopeless Generations) (Bang), 5

"I det skraa, øjenblændende Sollys" (In the Oblique, Dazzling Sunlight) (Paludan), 45

Joyce, James, 18
Jørgen Stein (Paludan), vii, ix, 11
  fluctuating popularity, 97–102
  and Paludan's other novels, ix, 59–77, 112n119
  reviews of, 99
  unevenness, viii–ix, 53–57, 97–102

Kafka, Franz, 52, 91
Kehler, Henning, 21

Kick Me in the Traditions (*Rend mig i traditionerne*) (Panduro), 98
Kierkegaard, Søren, 57
Kondrup, Johnny, 108n72
Kristensen, Sven Møller, 99
Kristensen, Tom, 64, 99, 125n227
Krøyer, Peder Severin, 56

Lady Chatterley's Lover (Lawrence), 57
Landet forude. Et Spil om Utopien (The Country Ahead. A Play about Utopia) (Eberlin and Paludan), 86
Larsen, Henrik, 43, 110n95
Lawrence, David Herbert, 57
Liar, The (*Løgneren*) (Hansen) and *En Vinter lang* (Winter Long), 65–67
von Linstow, Kai F., 83, 88–95, 120–121n206
literature
    essence of, viii–ix
    genesis of, vii–x, 102
Lundbo, Orla, 33, 36

Mai, Anne-Marie, 52, 111n104
Main Currents in Nineteenth-Century Literature (*Hovedstrømninger i det Nittende Aarhundredes Litteratur*) (Brandes), 80
Mann, Thomas, 5–6, 9, 11, 104–105n26
Markerne modnes (The Fields are Ripening), (Paludan), 69–75
    and *De vestlige Veje* (The Western Roads), 74–75
    and Paludan's other novels, ix, 76–77, 112n119
mediation
    external and internal, 49–51

narrator
    role of, 13–15, 52, 105n34
New York, 60, 62
Nielsen, Preben Erik, 27–28, 36, 99–101
Nordisk Fjer, 100, 126n231
Nøleren (The Delayer) (Rifbjerg), viii–ix

Oldenburg, Henrik, 79, 81, 86, 88, 95, 99

Paludan, Gerda Puggaard (mother), 79
Paludan, Hans Aage (brother), 79, 81–82, 95
Paludan, Jens Jacob (son), 85
Paludan, Julius (father), 79–80
Paludan, Vibeke (wife), 84
Panduro, Leif, 98, 124n220
Pedersen, Klaus Riskær, 100, 126n231
Petersen, Johannes, 100, 126n231
Politiken newspaper, 88–95
Proust, Marcel, viii

reading
    as creativity, ix–x
Reinvaldt, Henrik, 20–21, 23, 33
Remarque, Erich Maria, 97
Rifbjerg, Klaus, viii–ix, 98, 124n220
Rømhild, Lars Peter, 79, 81, 82, 98

Sarajevo, 3, 4, 53
Sartre, Jean-Paul, ix–x
Scavenius, Alice, 87, 120n198
Schou, Søren, 14, 33, 101–102, 105n34, 109n78
self-destructiveness
    and dehumanisation, 33
    and joie de vivre, 31–34, 40–41, 42–43, 49, 68
    see also suicide

140 Index

Seven Gothic Tales (Blixen), 37
"Shadow, The" (Andersen), 29
Skipper, Flemming, 88, 119n197
Skou-Hansen, Tage, 56–57
South America, 59, 74
Steinbeck, John, 97
Stengaard, Niels, 80,
 120–121n206, 123n214
Stuk (Stucco) (Bang), 34–35, 101
suicide, vii, 1–2, 9, 19, 32, 51–53,
 67–69, 88, 88–95, 95,
 101–102, 110n95, 126n231
 and family relationships, 2–4,
  21, 43
 in historical context, 2–4, 23,
  46, 48–49, 69, 76–77
 as consequence of loneliness,
  13, 36, 45, 48, 59, 76
 and anxiety for poverty, 17, 47
 in preference to prison, 42–43,
  48, 94
 as manifestation of self-oppression, 64, 72–75

and post-traumatic stress, 61–64
 see also self-destructiveness
Søgelys (Searchlight) (Paludan),
 61–64, 69
 and *Havoc* (Kristensen), 64
 and Paludan's other novels, ix,
  76–77, 112n119
Sørensen, Marianne, 4, 109n77

Terminal Innocence (*Den kroniske
 uskyld*) (Rifbjerg), 98

Ulysses (Joyce), 18
United States, The, xiv, 59, 61, 85

Violence and the Sacred (Girard),
 111n101

Zerlang, Martin, 20–21, 23, 33,
 98, 111n101